MW01170724

Social Action Heroes

Social Action Heroes

Unitarian Universalists
Who Are Changing the World

Michelle Bates Deakin

Skinner House Books
Boston

Printed in the United States

Cover and text design by Suzanne Morgan

print ISBN: 978-1-55896-646-8
eBook ISBN: 978-1-55896-647-5

6 5 4 3 2
13 12

Library of Congress Cataloging-in-Publication Data

Deakin, Michelle Bates.
  Social action heroes : Unitarian Universalists who are changing the world
/ Michelle Deakin.
      p. cm.
  ISBN 978-1-55896-646-8 (pbk : alk. paper)—ISBN 978-1-55896-647-5 (ebook)
  1. Social justice—Religious aspects—Unitarian Universalist Association. 2.
Unitarian Universalists—Biography. I. Title.
  BX9856.D43 2012
  261.8092'889132—dc23
  [B]
                                  2011025389

To my parents

Contents

Introduction

It's the first step that makes a difference.

For Paulie, it was renting a trailer. Janice quit her job. George booked a flight. Miranda didn't leave, even when she wanted to. Martha and Waitstill said yes. A group of children collected crayons.

Each were small steps. And all were righteous moments.

If you are trying to find a way to save the world—whether it's the whole word or a small corner of it—it's the first step that matters most. And then the step after that one.

This book profiles people who have made great strides in social justice work. It's easy to look at their accomplishments and imagine that they are extraordinary people whose efforts can't be matched. But each of these people is an ordinary person who started with a simple idea. "People think human rights work has to be about the extraordinary," says Karen Tse, who founded an international nonprofit to end torture and ensure due process rights for every citizen of the world. "But it's really the ordinary daily grunt work that ends up making a tremendous difference."

Few set out with a vision to found a nonprofit that will change the lives of thousands of people. But many have been inspired to take simple steps that lead toward great social justice work. Social change gains momentum with steady, consistent action.

Artemis Joukowsky's social justice work was inspired by his grandparents, Rev. Waitstill and Martha Sharp, who rescued hundreds of Jews, intellectuals, political leaders, artists, and children from the Nazis during World War II. As stunning as their heroism was, Joukowsky hopes their acts will inspire others, not overwhelm them or make them feel inferior and unable to match the Sharps' efforts. "Life is made of righteous moments, not grandiose moments," Joukowsky says. "The key part about my grandparents wasn't just one big moment. They made thousands of little choices that led up to the story that we now tell."

He tells his grandparents' story as an inspiration. And that is the intention of all the stories in this book. They showcase the worthwhile work of people committed to changing the world. And they invite readers to examine their own lives and ask what they can do. Once we understand the story of how one person creates change, we begin to see where there is room in our own lives to take righteous steps.

Each story is about a Unitarian Universalist individual, family, or group engaged in compelling social justice work. Some work within their own communities; others work across the world. Their stories, however, are not meant just for Unitarian Universalists. They can inspire anyone with a passion for justice, equity, and peace.

The book focuses on Unitarian Universalists because engaging in social justice work is, for many UUs, a compelling part of living their faith. Many feel morally obligated to act against injustice. That's how Paul Eisemann felt as he grew increasingly frustrated waiting for a volunteer opportunity to help New Orleanians after the levees broke and Hurricane Katrina flooded their city. "I was having a hard time reconciling my faith with inactivity," he said. What started as a one-time mission to help people rebuild there has grown for Eisemann into a calling to train youth and adults in how to respond to disasters with building and carpentry skills. He tells the volunteers he works with, "You get up in the morning, you brush your teeth, and you help another human being. . . . This is what living your faith looks, smells, and tastes like."

This book is intended for people interested in helping another human being without promoting their own faith agenda. As a group, UUs are not known to proselytize. They promote personal freedom, not personal faith.

These stories cover a wide range of social justice topics, from housing and hunger to environmentalism and anti-racism—although there are many other areas of need. This collection tells about ordinary people doing extraordinary things—people who have seen a need and felt called to fill it.

Some attempt to elevate one type of social justice work above another: service over charity, for example, or advocacy over service. However, there is no hierarchy in helping others. The best kind of social justice work is the kind that you feel called to do.

Katharine Esty tried painting low-income housing to fulfill her itch for social action, but she was a strategic planner and consultant. Her painting skills were poor, and she didn't have positive feelings about what she could contribute with a paintbrush in her hand. She needed to find a way to contribute her strengths. She helped found the Jericho Road Project, a highly successful nonprofit organization affiliated with First Parish in Concord, Massachusetts, that matches the skills of white-collar volunteers with nonprofits that need them.

Dr. Howard Thurman, a twentieth-century preacher and philosopher who was influenced by Mohandas Gandhi and who in turn influenced Rev. Dr. Martin Luther King Jr., gave us words to inspire any activist. Thurman believed in peaceful activism and in bringing all people together to worship and to work for peace. He said, "Don't ask yourself what the world needs. Ask yourself what makes you come alive and then go do that. Because what the world needs is people who have come alive."

What makes you come alive? What is your first step?

"This is what living your faith looks, smells, and tastes like."

Rebuilding New Orleans

Paul Eisemann watched New Orleans flood on TV in his rent-controlled apartment in the Boerum Hill neighborhood of Brooklyn in 2005. He tried to ignore newspaper images of broken levees, ravaged houses, and thousands of displaced families. But his eyes kept wandering back to pictures of the devastation that followed Hurricane Katrina.

"I remember seeing a twisted, snapped two-by-four and thinking, 'I know how to fix that. I'm a carpenter.' I know how to fix a two-by-four. And if you put enough together, you have a wall. And then a home," says Eisemann, known as Paulie, a self-taught contractor who makes his living restoring Brooklyn brownstones.

As he watched the waters engulf New Orleans, images of another urban catastrophe from four years before washed over him. While working in an office tower in midtown Manhattan, Paulie had stared down Sixth Avenue as the second World Trade Center tower collapsed after the 9/11 attacks. He knew what it was like to watch a city crumble. And he knew what it was like to feel a city recover. "I told myself, 'I can't sit this one out,'" he says.

He started calling volunteer organizations, asking what a skilled contractor could do. But in the chaos that followed Katrina, he couldn't get an answer. Paulie grew increasingly restless and frustrated waiting for an opportunity. He heard people at his church, First Unitarian Congregational Society in Brooklyn, wrestling with options that didn't materialize. "I was having a hard time reconciling my faith with inactivity," he says. "To talk about organizing a task force to explore the possibility of doing something—it's just talking about talking."

Paulie stumbled upon a contact at a New Orleans church who assured him that if he could get there, he'd find plenty of work waiting for him. That was all the encouragement he needed. He put the word out that he was looking for tools and books to take to New Orleans. Members of his church threw a pancake breakfast to raise money, and tools and books piled up. On Palm Sunday 2006 Paulie loaded them in a U-Haul trailer, hitched it to his fifteen-year-old Geo Prism, and drove south.

Just two hundred miles into his trip, he blew a tire, his car straining under the heavy load. Despite having a trailer full of tools, Paulie didn't have the right lug wrench to change a flat. He jerry-rigged a fix and drove on. But the closer he got to New Orleans, the more he doubted his mission. One night in Canton, Mississippi, he lay awake in a roadside motel, wondering, "Who do I think I am?" He accused himself of having "middle-aged white-man syndrome" for thinking he could just drive into a city and stick out a helping hand.

But in the light of the next day, that's what he did. Paulie drove the remaining two hundred miles of his trip and arrived outside First UU Church of New Orleans, where water had flooded the sanctuary, climbing four feet up the walls. The water stewed in the late summer heat and humidity for three weeks, demolishing the floor, the pews, two pianos, and the organ. Paulie surveyed the damage and felt a renewed sense of why he had come. "I'm here," he said. "Let's start fixin' shit."

Paulie stayed in New Orleans for three months on that first trip.

Since then, he's been back fourteen times, rebuilding the church, fixing homes, eating crayfish and shrimp, listening to jazz, and weaving himself into the city's spirit of recovery. He has trained hundreds of volunteers—adults and youth alike—in demolition and construction, and he has arranged the delivery of tons of donated materials to the Crescent City. In the process, Paulie has found himself to be more than a handyman or a contractor. He's a construction minister.

"I'm walking with these folks," Paulie says, his thick Brooklyn accent ensuring that he will never be mistaken for a native New Orleanian. "I've stood with them, and that will have a greater impact than making sawdust. I've used a lot of emotional caulk."

The *New York Times* called Eisemann "the Brownstone Whisperer." In a 2006 story, the newspaper chronicled the contractor's skill at listening to old houses and lovingly restoring them to their former glory.

New Orleanians, and the legions of volunteers who have come to rebuild the city, just call him Paulie.

Tall and wiry, Paulie keeps his brown hair cropped close and usually hidden under a well-worn New York Mets baseball cap. The pockets of his blue work shirt and canvas work pants are stuffed with the tools of his trade: a tape measure, a Sheetrock knife, a paint-can opener, pencils, and Camel cigarettes.

In April 2010 he has come to New Orleans for the fifteenth time since Katrina to lead a group of volunteers. As much as Paulie enjoys the hands-on work of building and repair, he's found his true calling in training others to measure, hammer, saw, and grout. "Anyone can do this stuff," Paulie says. "It ain't brain surgery."

He has led hundreds of volunteers, from teens to older adults, in gutting homes in the working-class Lower Ninth Ward of New Orleans, where waters from the broken levees left most of the neighborhood uninhabitable. Even five years later, some homes still have holes in the roofs, chopped from the inside by occupants trying to escape the rising waters. Paulie has led people in rebuilding the destroyed homes of local residents who were denied coverage by their insurance companies. And with thousands of hours of volunteer labor, he has helped rebuild the washed-out First UU Church of New Orleans.

"We've considered canonizing him," says Jyaphia Christos-Rodgers, of First Church. She wants to make him a saint to recognize his rebuilding work but also so they can call his wife, Cynthia Reynolds Eisemann, "St. Pauli's girl," she says with a wink. Christos-Rodgers hands out business cards that boast her unusual title, "Diva Chef." A longtime member of First Church, she has become cook and friend to the stream of volunteers who flow through.

As she describes how the volunteer energy has rebuilt the church, she lays out a delicious spread of the food she prepares to sustain them: yam bisque, greens, deviled eggs, roasted beets, and crawfish pasta. "We practice radical hospitality," she says. "We welcome the stranger as a friend."

Christos-Rodgers works alongside Quo Vadis Breaux, executive director of the Center for Ethical Living and Social Justice Renewal, housed on the second floor of First Church. It encompasses the volunteer center—a kitchen, rooms of bunk beds that can sleep up to fifty people, and classrooms that host workshops for out-of-town volunteers to talk about race, rebuilding, and culture. The Center for Ethical Living was created following Katrina by the three UU churches in Greater New Orleans: First Church, Community Church Unitarian Universalist in the city's Lakeview neighborhood, and North Shore Unitarian Universalist Society, across Lake Pontchartrain in LaCombe, Louisiana.

The center is a nonprofit group governed by the three churches and created to focus on the social justice needs of the greater New Orleans community. The ground floor of the partially rebuilt church houses an affordable childcare center and meeting space for community organizations. A large commercial kitchen is under construction. Breaux's hope is that the kitchen will be the new home of the New Orleans AIDS Task Force. Prior to Katrina, that group delivered more than eight hundred meals a day to people with HIV/AIDS. However, its kitchen was destroyed by the storm. Breaux is also in discussions with the One World Everybody Eats Foundation about establishing a community kitchen within the church. She hopes to call it the Welcome Home Café.

Although the commercial kitchen is still a work in progress, much of First Church has returned to life. Breaux points out the restored stained-glass windows, a gift from the UU Church of Arlington, Virginia, and marvels at the reopened sanctuary. Breaux is full of gratitude for the gifts from the volunteers who have rebuilt the sanctuary and the volunteer center. She also marvels at Paulie's inspiration to so many. As she reviews evaluations from volunteers about their time working through the Center for Ethical Living she finds that "almost to a person" people praise Paulie with "exclamation points." "Especially the youth groups," Breaux says. "He instructs them, and he trusts them. Teens really respond to that. It's wonderful to see."

Paulie deflects praise to the volunteers who've done the work. "Every inch of what's been done here has been imbued with love," he says.

The post-storm sanctuary smelled rotten. Receding floodwaters left a high-water mark four feet up the walls. The pews were totaled. The floor was buckled and mangy, covered in mold, mud, and mildew. The church's insurance policy provided coverage for the building's damaged roof but nothing for either the structure or the contents of the sprawling building, which covers an entire city block.

Today, the rebuilt sanctuary gleams. Paulie conceived of a creative way to hide the watermark on the tinted plaster walls. Recycling wood from the crumbling stage in the church's fellowship room, he built wainscoting around the perimeter of the sanctuary. It covers the line left by the standing water and serves as a reminder of how high the water rose.

From the vaulted ceiling, forty-two panels of billowing white cloth form a canopy above the sanctuary. They also hide areas where tiles were missing from even before the storm. Over the chancellery—

what was once called the altar in the building's former life as an evangelical church—the cloth on the ceiling is deep red.

The building's original stained-glass windows filter blue, green, and purple light into the sanctuary and onto the room's focal point: the newly laid floor. Rebuilding plans originally called for a bamboo surface, but in 2008, Paulie got a line on sixty tons of free ceramic tile. "Suddenly, the church leadership thought, 'Yeah. Tile sounds good,'" Paulie says.

Talking with buddies and contacts in New York, Paulie had learned about tons of leftover flooring material owned by Artistic Tile Co. Artistic had originally donated 120 tons of tile to the Women's Housing and Economic Development Corporation (WHEDco), a nonprofit that builds affordable housing in the South Bronx. WHEDco used half of the materials, leaving 60 tons of high-end discontinued tile sitting in a warehouse in Secaucus, New Jersey.

With his friend John Cramer, an energy-efficiency consultant, Paulie had been discussing how to get donated material down to New Orleans. Cramer had learned of the tile and asked Paulie if he could find a home for it. In a heartbeat, Paulie said yes. The bigger question remained, however: How to get sixty tons of tile from New Jersey to New Orleans?

The answer came in the form of another donation. Paulie sits on the board of the TUUL-Belt Ministry. Created and run by his friend Rev. Scott Sammler-Michael—the minister of the Accotink Unitarian Universalist Church in Burke, Virginia, and a former electrician—the TUUL-Belt Ministry helps UUs who have construction experience to respond rapidly to disasters in the United States.

TUUL-Belt provided $3,000 for one shipment of tile. And then Artistic volunteered to load and send two trucks of tile to New Orleans at no cost. Paulie wheeled, dealed, emailed, and telephoned to arrange the logistics. "It was a really long haul putting the details together, but big dreams cost the same as small ones, so dream big," he says.

Fate continued to smile on Paulie around the tile deal. He had hoped to be in New Orleans to see the tile delivered, but he couldn't afford a flight or the time to drive down. As luck would have it, an email from JetBlue airlines arrived in his inbox the day before the shipment, alerting him that he had qualified for a free round-trip flight. So Paulie booked it and was standing in front of First Church on the November day the truck pulled up with the tile. Watching the delivery arrive, Paulie says, "was the most beautiful sight in the world."

One load of tile was deposited on the sidewalk in front of First Church, and the remainder was unloaded at a former school—rendered unusable by the storm—that became a tile warehouse. One of Paulie's many phone calls had been to Mary Fontenot, executive director of All Congregations Together (ACT) New Orleans. ACT is dedicated to getting New Orleans homeowners back in their houses. It distributed the tile to local families. So did Lowernine.org, a group dedicated to rebuilding homes in the devastated Lower Ninth Ward. (Paulie was never a frequent committee member in the past, but he has found himself sitting on the boards of both ACT and Lowernine.org, in addition to the TUUL-Belt Ministry.) Homeowners across New Orleans have laid donated Artistic Tile in their kitchens and bathrooms.

The tile at First Church presented a job of a different scale. How does a church lay tons of donated tile of all different shapes and colors in its 3,500-square-foot sanctuary? The answer came in the form of Marcie Brennan, a New Orleans shipfitter, who spent six months designing the layout, cutting tile, and working on her hands and knees to lay it. Blue tile in the center aisle is accented by a fleur de lis, the New Orleans motif. Grey tile covers the bulk of the floor, with white squares comprising the chancellery floor.

But Brennan's pièce de résistance was in putting together a 2,000-square-foot walking labyrinth in the back of the sanctuary. Alone and in groups, church members and visitors come and go from the sanctuary, slowly, quietly walking the tile at a meditative pace. One tile nearest the church's front door is signed simply, "Anew 2009. Marcie Brennan."

A group of UUs from Boston has come to New Orleans in April 2010 to volunteer and attend Jazz Fest. Paulie patiently leads them through the how-tos of laying baseboard in the hallway of the church's offices and in grouting the chancellery tile.

The Boston crew includes Rev. Kim Crawford Harvie, senior minister of the Arlington Street Church, who has been leading volunteers from her congregation to New Orleans annually. Church member and architect Susie Nacco and her wife and children have come too. Nacco and Paulie have worked together for years to provide skilled volunteer labor and experience to rebuild the church. They gather at the home of Claudia Barker, a member of First UU and chair of the Greater New Orleans Unitarian Universalists Rebuilding and Revitalization campaign. Barker cherishes the lifelong ties she has made with volunteers, people she didn't even know before the storm. Barker's husband is the godfather of Nacco's youngest daughter. The children sprint though the Barkers' backyard, as Harvie, Nacco, and the Boston volunteers reconnect with Paulie and the local crew, making plans for volunteer work in the Lower Ninth Ward and Jazz Fest.

The finished areas of the church look professionally done, although they've been mostly completed with volunteer labor. "I try to get the same standard out of volunteers that I would out of myself," says Paulie, even though the volunteers don't work at the same speed as a professional crew.

Paulie says he has been transformed by watching New Orleanians receive the gifts of volunteer work. He has watched people stoically endure the loss of homes, the frustration of confronting the bureaucracy of insurance companies and the Federal Emergency Management Agency, the death of pets. But the generosity of strangers, Paulie says, makes people cry.

"People ask me what my stake is in all this," says Paulie. "My stake is in humanity. I always try to be clear that I'm here to be in service to the city. My spirit is being fulfilled in ways that I couldn't buy."

His New Orleans trips have meant a lot of separation between Paulie and his wife and son. Cynthia has joined him on occasion. However, she has a career in New York working with a specialty food trade association. His son, Luke, was fifteen when Paulie started making his trips to the Gulf, and would sometimes complain that Dad was gone too much. But Luke made some trips to New Orleans too.

"If it weren't for Cindy and Luke supporting the work that I do, I couldn't be doing it," says Paulie. "I give them credit for work that I do because they're part of my support team. They both understand this as part of what we do as members of our church and as members of the UU movement." He can't resist adding, "Sitting on your ass ain't movement."

His son is now enrolled in college, studying acting at New York University. It's a field Paulie admires. Before his Gulf Coast trips, Paulie dabbled in a part-time acting career. And his conversations still have a flair for the dramatic. At any opportunity, he slips into an Irish brogue, a guttural German accent, or a stern Russian.

Paulie's native tongue, however, is baseball. He's a lifelong Mets fan. His cell-phone voice mail message ends with a year-round cheer of "Let's go, Mets!" He seems to have every team clothing item a Mets fan could have. Cleaning up after a day of construction means slipping on a Mets T-shirt. If it's cold, he dons a Mets jacket and sips coffee from a Mets cup. And his favorite way to unwind in New Orleans during baseball season is to head to the ballpark. He's a regular at Zephyr Field, home of the New Orleans Zephyrs, the Triple-A affiliate of the Florida Marlins.

Paulie hadn't planned on becoming a Zephyrs fan—or on making fifteen trips to the Gulf Coast. He planned that first trip and never thought about coming back. But as he prepared to leave, people asked him when he would return. "So many people here are like family. I guess I've known them all my life, but I just met them four years ago," Paulie says. "There's a love that grows out of shared experience—the trauma of the loss and the resilience and hope of rebuilding. You become a part of it."

At the end of a day of grouting, Paulie sits on the porch of "the palace," a rambling shotgun home in the Garden District, smoking a Camel and drinking an Abita beer. The house belongs to First Church member Max Oeschger, who always has a room for Paulie when he's in New Orleans. A breeze carries a faint smell of oil in from the Gulf of Mexico. A week ago, an offshore British Petroleum platform blew up, spreading oil and a new catastrophe across the Gulf Coast states.

Paulie is thinking about Haiti, where a January earthquake leveled Port-au-Prince, killing more than 230,000 people and leaving more than a million homeless. He feels called to go and help them rebuild, and he's thinking of taking a crew of New Orleanians with him. Paulie knows the trauma of seeing another city devastated would be too severe for some Katrina survivors. But for others, he says, it would be the "completion of the circle of aid they have received."

It's different from after Katrina, when Paulie blindly called charitable organizations, looking for a way to help. Now he has his own network of rebuilders: Scott Sammler-Michael of the TUUL-Belt Ministry; Suzie Nacco, the Boston architect; John Cramer, who helped him with the donated tile. They're all talking, and they know they will find a way to get to Haiti together and begin rebuilding there.

Back in Brooklyn, Paulie is getting restless whispering to Brownstones. He feels compelled to whisper to volunteers who are rebuilding broken lives.

One of his prized possessions is the quilt stitched for him by the youth group of the First Parish UU Church in Needham, Massachusetts, that hangs over his living room couch. Each square of the quilt thanks Paulie for what he's taught the teens about construction and love and service: "Your commitment to helping people is inspirational." "Paulie, you are the man." "You are a gift to the universe." And for Paulie the Mets fan, one square says succinctly, "Yankees suck."

As Paulie hammers with volunteers, he preaches too, exhaling words of advice and inspiration. "You get up in the morning, you brush your teeth, and you help another human being," he tells them. Another day he says, "This is what living your faith looks, smells, and tastes like." Pushing grout around with a trowel, he says, "UUs are guided by freedom, reason, tolerance, and love. Being guided by those things, how do I find a way to give of myself that makes other human beings' lives better?"

Ideally, he'd like to find a way to make a living helping volunteers with the physical labor of reconstruction, work that leads to a spiritual transformation. It's a calling that's getting louder for Paulie, who has been forever changed by what he has given to New Orleans. "My spirit is being fulfilled in a way that I couldn't buy. We came here to teach, and we were educated. We came here to feed, and we were nourished. We were the recipients of what we thought we were giving. As you give, you are fulfilled."

The Center for Ethical Living & Social Justice Renewal
www.celsjr.org

Greater New Orleans Unitarian Universalists
www.gnouu.org

"To give is to dish out for oneself."

Creating Community Farms in an African Village

The Lynches' South African vacation was divided into three parts.

The first week, Tom and his thirteen-year-old daughter, Miranda, took a four-star safari through the wilds of the African bush. The second week they spent in the remote Zulu village of Inzinga. And the third week they toured in and around the coastal city of Cape Town.

It was the second week that changed their lives. And the lives of the villagers in Inzinga will never be the same either.

Witnessing the poverty and malnutrition in this Zulu village—in the midst of hospitality like none that Tom and Miranda had ever experienced—altered the course of Miranda's teen years, Tom's career, and the villagers' nutrition and educational opportunities.

As they waited at the Johannesburg airport for their flight back to Atlanta, Tom and Miranda registered a domain name for a new charitable foundation. Miranda decided to call the organization *Isipho*. That's the Zulu word for "gift"—and the name a three-year-old Inzinga villager gave to Miranda. In return for the villagers' gift of opening their eyes and hearts, the daughter and father vowed to find a way to give back an isipho of their own. They wanted to create a means for villagers to get the tools they needed to grow crops and build schools.

Before they left for South Africa in May 2008, Miranda and Tom could never have predicted the outcome of their visit to Inzinga especially since during their first night there, Miranda cried and begged her father to take her home.

First, there was the long and harrowing journey to the village. The previous week had been a dream. Tom had won a luxury safari at a fundraising auction for Miranda's private school. Miranda's mother stayed home while Tom and Miranda embarked on the father-daughter trip of a lifetime. On the safari, they saw giraffes and rhinos, elephants and lions. At night, they slept in storybook tents. Zulu guides catered sumptuous buffets of wild game.

When the safari came to an end, Tom rented a car, and they drove to Durban, the port city in the province of KwaZulu-Natal. From there, they drove two hours to the end of the last paved road in the regional capital, Impendle. It was a town of three streets, a few stores and bars, a health clinic, a police station, and a post office. Cows wandered the roads. From there, things began to get really rural.

Tom drove them twenty-five miles over unpaved, bumpy roads, careful to avoid the potholes and gullies, kicking up a cloud of dust behind them. He drove faster then he would have liked, struggling to keep up with Samantha Rose, who was leading them from Durban to Inzinga. Tom and Miranda had found Samantha before they left Atlanta, as they searched for a way to balance their luxury safari with a week of service. Tom had emailed the Durban Unitarian Congregation to enquire about where they might stay, and Samantha had responded and arranged for them to experience life in a remote South African township. They drove around the flat-topped Impendle Mountain, through a valley, over the bumpy, sandy terrain, and across a bridge, when Inzinga finally came into view. Round white huts with thatched roofs dotted the dusty landscape. As they pulled up to the hut of the Zuma family, people came into focus.

Nonjabulo Zuma was cutting firewood with her sisters. Trying to be both chivalrous and a gracious guest, Tom began to help with the sweaty, heavy work. He cut his leg twice chopping wood but soldiered on to help his hosts. Miranda pitched in too, wiping sweat from her freckled face as she strained to pile wood.

The Zumas welcomed the Lynches to their home, preparing a feast for their guests. Sitting on grass mats on the earthen floor, the families ate bread and beans and a fresh-killed chicken from the cast-iron pot.

After dinner, Tom and Miranda stepped outside and looked up at a sky like they had never seen. At the high altitude, with no ambient light, they felt they could reach out and touch the Milky Way and the stars above them. Tom was moved and at peace. "I felt a strong sense of how cluttered and plastic and superficial our lives are. We don't realize what we've given up. That kind of meal and this sky. It's a hard life they live, but it hit me how much we've lost and the things that we can't buy."

Miranda, however, was not feeling her father's transcendent joy. When she and Tom retreated to their hut for the night, she began to sob. In twenty-four hours, she'd gone from a lavish safari to seeing her own dinner killed and eating it in a mud hut. "This is too much for me," she said. "It's much too hard. I can't cut wood. I can't do this. Promise we can leave tomorrow."

Tom was unsure what to do. They'd arrived with hoses and shovels, books, crayons, and pencils for the school, and a promise to visit and help for the week. How could they pick up and leave after just twelve hours? How could he stay with Miranda in such despair?

He comforted her the best he could and hoped that in the light of day, he could help turn her attitude around. He didn't have to. Three-year-old Amahle did.

The next morning, Miranda emerged from the hut to find Amahle waiting for her. The daughter of Nonjabulo, Amahle had hidden behind her mother's skirt at dinner. But this morning, she'd had an attitude change too. Miranda unpacked her soccer ball, and the girls began to kick it back and forth. In Zulu, Miranda could say only one word, *Sawubona*, or "hello." But soon she was saying, "Go get it." And she was laughing.

For a week, Amahle and Miranda were glued at the hip. Holding hands. Miranda carrying Amahle. But Amahle never did learn to say Miranda. Instead, she called her *Isipho*, "gift." They were isipho to each other.

Miranda began to read to the children in the school, and Tom distributed the hoses and shovels and helped with the physical work in the village. Many facets of village life troubled him. The village has few adult men. Most have gone to cities to work so they can send money home. Many have been lost to AIDS. KwaZulu-Natal has the highest HIV/AIDS infection rate in the world. As elders die of the disease, so does their knowledge of farming.

Poverty and apartheid has also ravaged the villagers' ability to farm. Under apartheid, 80 percent of the native population was restricted to less than 13 percent of the land. According to the Alternative Information and Development Centre (AIDC), a South African social justice agency, apartheid law led to farmland overuse, soil erosion, and low productivity. Farming families began to turn to nonagricultural employment. Knowledge and equipment deteriorated, along with farm productivity and nutrition. In Inzinga, like many villages, poverty impeded the villagers' ability to buy seeds, equipment, and fencing. In 2008, residents subsisted primarily on beans and corn meal.

With Amahle on her hip, Miranda began to fall in love with the people of Inzinga. Each day, she went to the village school, playing games with the children and teaching them their ABCs. The children's passion to learn impressed her. They had none of the props and tools of an American school. The elementary school children had a "grimy ABC chart," she says. The middle-schoolers had a poster with vocabulary words written in large block letters: DISEASE, IMMUNE, PAMPHLET, HIV, AIDS, POLLUTION.

Tom began working with women planting crops at the village's center for OVCs—orphaned and vulnerable children. It's for children who have lost their parents, typically to AIDS or tuberculosis. Each year, the women planted potatoes. But year after year of planting was not leading to many successful crops. Free-range cattle and chickens were trampling the plants. The women's hard work yielded little.

"A light went on for us," says Tom. "These folks wanted to make their lives better, and they were working hard. They just didn't know the best way, and they didn't have the tools." With the shovels they had brought, Tom and Miranda helped plant potatoes. "They were excited to have the tools. They had a lot of pride and energy. We saw that with the right tools, they could do this for themselves. You take away people's pride and dignity when you make them dependent on your gifts," says Tom. But these were gifts they could use.

With planting done and school lessons taught, Tom and Miranda became wedding guests. Nonjabulo took them to the neighboring village for a two-day traditional Zulu extravaganza. They danced and sang; Tom drank from the communal bucket of beer; and they feasted on cow and goat. With every hour of the celebration, they felt more connected to their friends in Inzinga. The idea of leaving gave them lumps in their throats.

The day they left the village, Nonjabulo asked, "Will you be coming back?"

Miranda, the girl who wanted to leave on the first night, answered her. "We're coming back." Driving the dusty road back toward Durban, Miranda was adamant. "We're not just driving away. We got a lot out of being there. We can help them. We're coming back."

On the plane from Cape Town to Johannesburg before their flight home, Tom and Miranda uploaded photos from their South African odyssey to a laptop and watched a slideshow of where they'd been. They shared an iPod—each with one earbud in an ear—and listened to U2 sing "Miracle Drug": "Of science and the human heart / There is no limit / There is no failure here sweetheart / Just when you quit / I am you and you are mine / Love makes nonsense of space and time." Tom and Miranda wept.

"We have to find a way to stay connected," Miranda told her dad. "We have to find a way to get more tools and fencing."

They talked about reaching out to nonprofits that might help Inzinga. But Miranda asked, "Why not start our own? We'll call it Isipho."

Tom opened his laptop again in the Johannesburg airport and registered the domain name: www.isipho.org.

Sheri Lynch had missed her husband and only child for three weeks. She'd long been anticipating their return and relished the chance to see their pictures and souvenirs. She never expected they'd walk in with a new nonprofit and a job for her.

On the flight from Johannesburg to Atlanta, Isipho began to take shape. Without even having heard of the new venture, Sheri was appointed executive director.

Sheri works as a professional organizer and has a background in nonprofit management. For many years, she ran burn camps—programs for children recovering from serious burns. Tom and Miranda were counting on her experience and her skills.

Tom began preparing to tackle the marketing and public relations for Isipho. He has worked as a corporate marketing and advertising executive in Atlanta for decades.

And Miranda has been the group's public face and what Tom calls the "emotional anchor" of Isipho.

The family began to hold regular business meetings to run the nonprofit. They came up with guiding philosophies that were inspired by their Unitarian Universalist faith. They based their new organization on the first Principle of Unitarian Universalism —"to affirm and promote the inherent worth and dignity of every person."

Their goal was to raise money to supply the people of Inzinga with farm tools, fencing, and seeds to help them plant community gardens. They also wanted to provide greater educational opportunities for the children there. "We knew that they did not need a handout, something that replaces their poverty with dependence," says Miranda. "They needed a hand up. Just a little help getting started."

The Lynches began a long process of educating themselves on how to find the right tools and seeds for the village. They contacted Cedara Agricultural College in KwaZulu-Natal to learn what kinds of crops Inzinga could support and what kind of training the college could provide.

They set their sights on a year of fundraising so they could return to Inzinga in 2009 with tools, money, and training. The Lynches began to tap all their friends and family for donations. Miranda told her story to their church, the Unitarian Universalist Congregation of Atlanta, and hosted a fundraising dinner there. The family hosted a wine-tasting party. Donations began to mount. By June, they totaled $13,000, and the Lynches were ready to return to Inzinga with their gifts.

Over the year, during family business meetings and while networking with others, the Lynches tried to learn about the best farming techniques to help the village. "My mother asked me, 'What do you know about gardening?'" Sheri says. "But we knew what we wanted to accomplish, and we knew people would teach us how."

Miranda met with the chief of staff of the humanitarian organization CARE, based in Atlanta, and the family spoke with experts from the Heifer Project, the Hunger Project, and even people running local farmers' markets. They learned through the United Nations Food and Agriculture Organization that a garden the size of a door can provide food for a family for a year.

In August 2009, Tom and Miranda returned to Inzinga. It felt like going home. Little Amahle was reunited with her isipho, Miranda, and the wide, warm smile of Nonjabulo welcomed them back. Sheri stepped for the first time into the world that had so captivated her daughter and husband.

They arrived with gardening tools, seeds, and fencing materials. The Lynches purchased materials in South Africa to keep the money within the local economy. Some of the donated funds went to providing training in sustenance gardening at Cedara College for twenty villagers. The Lynches and the villagers rolled up their sleeves and began to hoe the brown earth.

Together, they planted five hundred square yards of community gardens and forty family gardens, with spinach, onions, cabbage, beet root, squash, carrots, kale, peppers, beans, peas, and chard. Nonjabulo became the manager of Isipho in the village, working with the Department of Agriculture in South Africa and with the Lynches in Atlanta. She watched as the crops grew. One community garden planted at a crèche (or kindergarten) produced enough vegetables to sell, raising money to buy books.

The sale of the harvest prompted a letter to the Lynches from the principal of the Inzinga Primary School, Florence Thandiwe Nxumalo. She wrote, "God gave us a blessing that we will never forget that is Isipho. You wipe away our tears."

The proceeds of those first crops provide a glimpse of the self-sustainability that Isipho and the villagers are looking for. "If we're still doing this in Inzinga ten years from now, we will have failed," says Tom. "Ideally, we'll show up in Inzinga five or six years from now, and they won't need us. Then we'll go across the valley to another village."

And the Lynches hope they can pass their template for aiding Inzinga along to other groups working in other villages and other countries.

"To give is to dish out for oneself." It's a Zulu phrase that has come true for the Lynches. Miranda, Sheri, and Tom believe that Isipho has transformed their family and their lives.

After starting Isipho, Tom began to experience growing dissatisfaction with his corporate marketing career. By day, he was engineering ways to sell unhealthy snacks to American children, many of whom were already overweight. By night, he was brainstorming with Sheri and Miranda about combating income inequality and hunger. When his supervisor approached him about laying off some of his staff, Tom decided to write himself into the layoff plan.

He then started a new business with a social conscience. Worthwhile Wine Co. imports South African wines to the United States. Tom's mission is to import top-quality wines that are produced by fair-trade, sustainable wineries.

He organized the company according to a corporate structure that is increasingly attractive to companies interested in social responsibility. Worthwhile Wines is a B corporation. Unlike traditional S or C corporations that are legally obligated to produce as much money as possible to reward shareholders, a B corporation takes into consideration a company's impact on people and the environment, as well as profits. Taking into account people, the planet, and profits, B corporations are also known as "triple bottom line" companies.

"We are importing only wines from companies that go about the business of making great wines with an eye toward taking better care of the earth and those with whom they interact," says Tom. That means they are involved in a number of sustainable practices, including organic farming, fair trade, responsible water usage, waste reduction, and preservation of the surrounding habitat. He also favors companies in the Black Enterprise Empowerment program, which provides equity, training, and opportunity to black South Africans who were disadvantaged during apartheid. This program gives workers ownership and influence in the wineries they have often lived and worked on for generations. Worthwhile Wines also buys carbon offsets to balance the environmental impact of shipping wine from South Africa to the United States.

As Tom switched careers, Miranda switched schools. She decided to leave Paideia, the private school she had attended for seven years. She enrolled in the Ben Franklin Academy, a school with a half-day academic schedule combined with a work program. That allows Miranda to go to school in the mornings and work on Isipho in the afternoons. It also gives her more time for her other passions—dance, teaching dance to young children, and filmmaking.

Miranda had returned from her August 2008 visit to Inzinga with a renewed interest in school. She got herself organized and committed to academics in a way she never had before. After seeing the conditions in the Inzinga schools, she says, "I understood how good I have it and how lucky I am."

"The impact of Isipho on us has been massive," says Tom. "Our whole family is different."

Prior to having their own family nonprofit, they had never held family board meetings. Isipho was incorporated in December 2008. In March 2009, it was certified as a 501(c)(3) nonprofit. The family holds Isipho meetings every other week.

In 2010, Sheri and Tom celebrated their twenty-fifth wedding anniversary. Married while students at the University of Southern Mississippi, they'd always vowed they would never work together. But Isipho changed that. "We've had a few Isipho meetings that have dissolved into tears and stomping out the room but not many," says Sheri.

They have each evolved into their own role in Isipho. Tom and Miranda like the large, conceptual ideas. Sheri works out the details. Miranda blogs about Isipho and about the experience of being a teenage entrepreneur working with her parents. She has grown to love speaking about Isipho. Annual visits to Africa have become highlights of each year.

In the fall of 2009, the *Atlanta Business Chronicle* named Miranda one of its "20 under 20" leaders of the year. At the awards ceremony, the emcee asked her a single question: "There is hunger everywhere. Why Inzinga?"

"I didn't really choose them," Miranda responded. "People are people. But these are the ones who inspired me."

In April 2010, Nonjabulo came to America for the first time. She became the second person in her village ever to visit America and the first in her family to ride in a plane. "When I am here, I am in my second home," she says.

Nonjabulo is a soft-spoken woman of twenty-eight with a

ready smile. She dresses in the long skirts favored by the women in her village. She's missing her daughter, Amahle, and her fiancé on her three-week sojourn. But her days are full of new experiences to distract her from thoughts of those she's left in Inzinga. She's learning about the hometown of the family that has helped to change her village.

She visits the Lynches' church and speaks at a fundraising dinner there, and she addresses the students at Miranda's school. She takes in the tourist sites—the zoo and the aquarium. Nonjabulo tours the CNN headquarters and learns to bowl and play minigolf. And she prepares to help host the first major Isipho fundraiser, Celebrating Hope 2010.

At the Trolley Barn, a renovated Victorian train station in Atlanta's Inman Park neighborhood, ninety guests have gathered, nibbling on bobotie rolls, pastries filled with curried beef and apricots, and akara, black bean cakes seasoned with garlic and spice. Worthwhile Wines are flowing, and Nonjabulo graciously and patiently answers questions from the guests, who've paid $100 each to attend the elegant garden party. Around the edges of the courtyard under the blazing Atlanta heat of early May, guests bid on sports memorabilia, dinners, and gift baskets. Framed photos of Miranda's portraits of Inzinga's children are a big draw. So is the high-ticket prize of the evening: two six-day photo safari packages, the same safari that set the wheels of Isipho in motion.

As the guests sit for dinner, Miranda rises to address them. She's gained a new confidence and poise as Isipho's spokeswoman. Her ginger hair is pulled back in a ponytail. Her green eyes sparkle above her dark eyeliner and her freckles. Miranda's full-length pink and orange sundress flows as she walks to the podium. She thanks the guests for coming. "*Ngiyabonga.* Thank you." And she welcomes her friend and role model, Nonjabulo. "She's smart, funny, talented, witty, courageous, and very cute," says Miranda.

Nonjabulo swallows her shyness and steps onto the stage. She tells the crowd how impressed she was when Tom and Miranda arrived and began to help them chop wood. No one has seen more than she has how the village has changed as she has helped to implement the Isipho vision. Describing the impact of Isipho, Nonjabulo pauses, smiles widely, and says, "Everything is wow!" She sees a future for Inzinga as an independent village that can raise crops and sell them to buy the things they need.

Nonjabulo's dark eyes sparkle, full of love that she is not shy about expressing. "I've never seen a woman her age like Miranda. I love her." And on behalf of her village, she acknowledges the donations. "I want to thank you all for your time and your contribution. We love you."

The Soweto Street Beat, a South African troupe, comes to the stage to drum and dance. Echoing the Zulu proverb, the leader tells the audience, "Thank you for helping Africa, because one day Africa will help you."

The evening netted just over $10,000. "Pretty good for a first event in a major economic slump," says Sheri. The money will go a long way toward establishing more gardens in Inzinga and training more families in farming them.

Despite creating and developing Isipho during a crippling recession in the United States, the Lynches are determined to move forward. Many international relief organizations have pulled up stakes from South Africa. Even with the devastating poverty and hunger in areas such as KwaZulu-Natal, South Africa is the most prosperous country in Africa. Yet the gap between its rich and its poor is among the world's greatest.

So each August, the Lynches will return to plant and to visit with their second family. They will also return this year for Nonjabulo's wedding. When talk turns to wedding planning, Miranda sounds less like a nonprofit entrepreneur and more like the fifteen-year-old she is. "Zulu weddings are incredible!" she says, her big eyes opening wider. "It's a like a three-day party. It'll be awesome!"

Isipho
www.isipho.org

"You can see the transformation of the children unfold before your eyes."

Welcoming Children Lost in Foster Care

Two extra large pizzas. Two orders of onion rings. Two orders of wings. And two large fries. No leftovers.

That's the standing order for Friday night dinner for the Stewart family: Five boys, two dads, and four dogs.

Ten years ago, Stillman White and Greg Stewart adopted their first child. Three-year-old Allen, born three weeks premature with fetal alcohol syndrome and a cocaine addiction, had been moving from foster home to foster home his whole short life.

Six months later, baby David arrived. Allen's biological brother, he'd been abandoned at the hospital after birth. He joined the family at two-and-a-half weeks.

At nearly the same time David joined them, Arthur arrived. Just seven years old, Arthur had already lived in fifteen foster placements and experienced the crushing disappointment of three failed adoptions, as potential parents changed their minds.

Then another pair of brothers arrived. Javonte, seven, and Dionte, six, had been in twelve previous placements. They had never received a present in their lives. They didn't even know their birthdays. Neither boy was toilet trained or could use silverware. Stillman and Greg arranged to meet them for the first time at a Los Angeles playground. Javonte saw them coming. He jumped off his swing, ran across the playground, and threw himself into Stillman's arms. "Papi!"

In just two years, they became a family of seven.

Many adoptive parents are very specific about the type of child they will bring into their family. But Stillman and Greg put no conditions on whom they would adopt. They didn't ask for an infant. Or a white child. "We never set out to have five boys or to have a family of color," said Stillman, who like Greg is white. Arthur is Latino, and David, Allen, Javonte, and Dionte, are African American. "We like to say that they picked us. We didn't pick them."

The dads describe their parenting as a calling—an irresistible urge to provide a loving home for children who wouldn't otherwise have one: high-risk, hard-to-place children lost in the foster-care system. It's likely that these boys would have either continued to bounce from foster home to foster home or been placed in a residential institution where children are warehoused like so many overstocked appliances.

"I came to realize that my calling in life was to cross paths with five boys that I would otherwise have never met and share my life with them," says Greg.

Stillman, a stay-at-home parent for ten years, says, "I feel I'm doing what I'm supposed to be doing with my life."

Both Stillman and Greg believe their parenting has lead to their spiritual transformation. And both are open to adopting more children.

"The decisions we make may not always be rational," says Greg. "But they come from our hearts and our sense of urgency that the world is broken, and we have a limited time on earth to make it better."

On July 4, 2010, Stillman and Greg celebrated their thirtieth anniversary. On that night thirty years ago, stuck in traffic on Lake

Shore Drive, they had watched Independence Day fireworks explode over Chicago.

Since that electric night, several signs indicated that Stillman and Greg eventually would adopt. But it took two decades for them to realize it. The pair met in Columbus, Ohio. Greg was home from college for the summer, working at the same veterinary supply store as Stillman, who had come to Ohio to put some distance between himself and his conservative, strict Baptist family in Michigan.

They decided to move to Chicago together so Greg could return to school. With the help of Greg's father, they found a house-sitting gig and began to put down roots there. "I thought I was moving in with a rock star," laughs Stillman, who still expresses some surprise that Greg would eventually become a Unitarian Universalist minister. At the time, Greg was singing and playing keyboards in a Christian rock band.

Greg persuaded Stillman to attend school as well. He first enrolled in a community college, and then joined Greg at the University of Illinois at Chicago, studying at the Jane Addams College of Social Work. His interest in helping others was his response to his memories of how his family had been treated by social workers when he was a child.

Stillman was raised on a Michigan farm. When his father was just thirty-three, he fell off a barn and broke his back. With no insurance, the family went "from middle class to no class," Stillman said. In the days before food stamps, he and his five brothers and sisters were raised on government-issued food: blocks of cheese, peanut butter, cornmeal, and rice. The family fished, and his mother gardened. And social workers dropped in to assess their situation. "I hated the way the social service people treated us," says Stillman. "They treated us like crap. I knew I wanted to make things better for other people."

As Stillman began his career in social work, Greg felt a call to the ministry. Like Stillman, he had been raised a Baptist, and his father was a minister. While at the University of Chicago, he found an internship at the Second Unitarian Church.

Stillman had hoped to find a job working with seniors but couldn't land a position. Greg encouraged him to work with kids instead. Stillman accepted a position at the Paulina House, a youth residential treatment facility, part of the Maryville network of youth services, a Catholic organization run by the Archdiocese of Chicago. Stillman fell in love with the work. He abandoned his ideas about working with the elderly and spent fourteen years in Chicago working with children in group homes and foster care.

Some of the teenage boys who lived at Paulina House asked Stillman to take them to church. Stillman could see no reason not to, so he assembled a group of boys one Sunday and drove them in a van to a nearby church. He quickly found that they were not welcome. Church members cast steely glances at the group of inner-city boys, who stood out among the buttoned-down crowd.

He tried taking the boys to three different churches. But each week, parishioners avoided them. And at the end of each service, the minister or the youth coordinator would approach Stillman and suggest other churches they might attend that were more set up for kids. They were kind, but their message was always the same: "Go to a different church. We don't want you here."

Meanwhile, Greg was an intern at Second Unitarian. He suggested that Stillman bring the boys there. Stillman and the eight boys from Paulina House were welcomed with open arms. Word began to get around to some of the other Maryville homes that there was a church that accepted at-risk inner-city kids. And some of Stillman's counterparts began bringing youth from their residential homes too. Greg was running the children's chapel, where he had started the Way Cool Sunday School. Instead of sitting and talking about Sunday school topics, the children were out doing them: recycling, working at food pantries, moving, and doing. The program grew from a dozen white children to nearly one hundred, of many races and religions.

"They especially loved the coffee hour," Stillman recalls with a laugh, noting that the children thrived in the atmosphere of freedom, tolerance, and respect. The church began to include the Maryville youth in youth conferences, parties, and overnights. "We really started seeing potential in the kids," says Stillman. "They weren't bad kids. They were being treated like human beings at church, and they didn't act up."

Stillman and Greg may have ushered these children into the church, but the minister and members of Second Unitarian made sure that they stayed. Rev. Charlie Kast was a foster parent himself, and over his lifetime had opened his home to more than eighty children. At one service, Kast asked the congregation of 150 if anyone would like to go to the Maryville homes to mentor these at-risk youth who had become a part of their church community. After the service, 75 people signed up. "They were rough kids, but they loved the church. It really changed the community," Greg says. "And it really changed Stillman and me."

During this period, Stillman got a call from one of the boys he had worked with at Maryville. He was turning eighteen and aging out of the system that had given him his home, his guidance, his food, his entire life's structure. With his approaching birthday and impending adulthood, he would have nowhere to go. Stillman and Greg invited John to come live with them. They helped him find a job and to enroll in community college.

And they both began to wonder: What if they had been involved in the lives of these at-risk children earlier? In the backs of their minds, a seed was planted.

But life in the ministry involved significant uprooting. Greg received a call to become the minister of religious education in an Ohio church, so the couple returned to the state where they'd met. During their three years in Shaker Heights, Greg shaped the Sunday school program, and Stillman worked at a treatment center for mentally ill children. Stillman began to investigate obtaining a license so they could become foster or adoptive parents. But he kept hitting roadblocks, unable to find any social workers willing to work with two gay dads.

Adopting in Ohio became a moot point, however, when Greg

was asked to become minister of religious education at the Neigh-borhood Unitarian Universalist Church in Pasadena, California. Soon after they arrived, Eddie, another boy from Maryville, called. They invited him to fly out to California, and as with John, they helped him learn to navigate the world outside a home for teenage boys. Again, they wondered, what if we could have worked with these boys when they were younger?

One Sunday, Greg preached to the congregation about the foster-care crisis in America, suggesting that congregants find ways to become involved in the lives of one of the tens of thousands of children without a permanent home. In the congregation that day was a social worker who worked in the California foster-care sys-tem. He approached Greg after the service and asked him, "Have *you* ever thought about adopting?"

Greg told him that he and Stillman had been thinking about it for years. Stillman and Greg discussed the proposition, and they agreed the time had come. The social worker promptly arranged a visit for Greg and Stillman to see some children who were in need of adoption.

On that first visit in 1999, Greg and Stillman drove to the heart of South Central Los Angeles to visit a foster family caring for two brothers, aged six and seven. The boys' foster mother had expressed no interest in adopting the boys. That is, until she had a visit from two gay men who wanted to give them a home. Under California state law, foster families have the right of first refusal in adopting, so when she expressed an interest in the boys, Greg and Stillman could no longer consider adopting them.

The boys did, however, have a three-year-old younger brother, Allen, living in another Los Angeles home. Greg and Stillman adopted him. Six months later, Stillman became a stay-at-home dad. And new boys kept joining the family. Over the next two years, they adopted David, Arthur, Javonte, and Dionte.

Greg and Stillman believe it's important to be open and public about the things that they believe in. "Jesus' ministry was public," says Greg. "I'm trying to do what Jesus did. It's important to model authentic faith."

As part of his public ministry, Greg had been open about advocating for the rights of same-sex couples. He and Stillman have had three very public weddings to promote the cause of equal marriage. Their first was in a synagogue in West Hollywood. Along with about one hundred other same-sex couples, they were married in a mass wedding under California's first domestic partnership program.

Their second wedding took place at the Neighborhood Church in Pasadena in 2000, to raise awareness of California ballot initiative Proposition 22, which would define marriage as only between a man and a woman. Their new son Allen put on his first suit to attend his fathers' wedding.

Their third wedding was in San Francisco in 2008, on the night before Election Day, when Proposition 8 was on the ballot. It was held in the First Unitarian Universalist Church of San Francisco, where Greg was senior minister. Their five sons attended. So did Eddie and about five hundred others—friends and members of the church and the community. The ballot measure banning same-sex marriages passed. However, Greg and Stillman, as well as the other same-sex couples who were married during a six-month period prior to the November election, still had valid marriages under California state law. (At the time of the wedding, Stillman also legally changed his name from Stillman White to Stillman Stewart so that everyone in the family could have the same last name.)

Just as they have been public with their weddings to promote same-sex marriage rights, Stillman and Greg have been public about their adoptions to help publicize the need for loving homes for foster children. That's why they agreed to permit two documentary filmmakers to follow the lives of their family for five years.

"We knew we had a very special story, but the reason we share it is to expose people to the foster-care crisis in America and to encourage people of liberal faith to act on their beliefs," says Greg.

"We want them to consider adoption or foster care or some other way to inject themselves into a child's life."

Their story had attracted the attention of several television networks, which had approached them about filming their family. The Stewarts always refused these requests. Things changed, however, when they were approached by two members of the Neighborhood Unitarian Universalist Church in Pasadena while Greg was serving there. The Stewarts didn't believe the networks shared their mission of promoting the adoption of at-risk children. But they trusted fellow church members and husband-wife-filmmakers Mark Nealey and C Roebuck Reed.

Nealey and Reed began filming the Stewart family in 2002. Nealey's background was in film editing and directing. Reed is trained as a cultural anthropologist. "This was my dream—to do an ethnographic-style documentary," says Reed. "We knew it was going to be a good story. But they also turned out to be fabulous parents."

In the opening scene, Stillman sits by a Los Angeles pool with Greg, as the two white men watch their sons, five boys of color, splashing in the water, calling out "Papa" and "Daddy." Stillman laughs and recounts a conversation he's just overhead between two older women at the pool who were observing their family. "Uh-oh!" one woman said. "There must be something wrong here."

The movie follows the family through their four homes. Despite what the women by the pool thought, the film depicts the Stewarts as doing something very right. Nealey and Reed recorded the family coming together, and they saw the children change. "You can see the transformation of the children unfold before your eyes," Reed says. "That is the power of love. That is what the film shows."

Reed released the movie, *Preacher's Sons*, in the summer of 2009. Nealey had completed the editing of the film in late 2007. But four months after they finished the film, he died of a recurrence of cancer. After his death, Reed says, she went into a tailspin.

Reed put the release and distribution of the film on hold, while she and her adult daughters, Maia Nealey Reed and Riva Nealey Reed, who had also worked on the film, grieved over Nealey's death. In July 2009, Reed left her California house, bought a used motor home and headed to Montana and South Dakota on a self-guided spiritual retreat. "I needed to figure out my next act," she says.

Reed decided to launch a grassroots effort to promote the film. She contacted Rev. Dr. Lee Barker. Although he had gone on to be president of Meadville Lombard Theological School in Chicago, Barker had been minister of the Pasadena church when Reed's family joined, and he acted as an advisor on the film. Barker wrote a letter of recommendation for the film to ministers in areas of the country where Reed planned to tour. She allows churches to show the film for free if they allow her to come sell the DVD.

Reed also has screened the film at colleges and universities. For example, she showed *Preacher's Sons* in three parts at an occupational-therapy class at the University of Southern California. Students watched as the film depicted the family moving to Greg's new jobs—from Pasadena to Grand Rapids, Michigan, to Reno, Nevada, and finally to San Francisco. Reed watched as students who were initially opposed to gay adoptions began to soften their positions. One young man told her, "I know my pastor still says it's a sin, but you have to admit, these kids are doing really well."

Reed also has prepared a program for social workers who work with same-sex couples preparing for foster care and adoption. She offers them a training program and a study guide. Parts of the movie were also featured in a November 2009 segment of *In the Life*, a PBS series that explores lesbian, gay, bisexual, and transgender issues.

Stillman and Greg have watched the movie with the boys, both at home and at a public screening in Pasadena. To his family, Greg says, *Preacher's Sons* is more than a film. "It's a testimony that if you're open to possibility and have a faith that says yes more than it says no, great things can happen.

"We certainly didn't start out with this grand scheme," Greg continues. "A need was put before us that we could meet, and we chose to say yes. That's where the real power in a spiritual life is—being able to say yes."

Greg and Stillman have said yes to the need. But they've also had to say no to the kids. Discipline and structure are key to life in the Stewart household.

The boys have been raised with sticker charts and chores—high expectations and low tolerance for misbehavior. "That's not where that plate goes," Greg says to David as he puts his plate down next to the TV on Friday pizza night. David grudgingly picks it up and carries the plate to the kitchen sink, keeping the living room clean. D—as Dionte is called—had straightened and vacuumed the living room earlier in the day as part of his weekly routine.

Having worked in group homes for fourteen years, Stillman has picked up many tools of the trade. And he embodies a calmness that helps him weather the daily storms of their four teenage sons. Arthur is now seventeen. Javonte, called Jo, is sixteen. D is fifteen. Allen is fourteen, and David is ten. "They've never shown me anything I had never seen before," says Stillman. "But I did used to go home at the end of the day," he jokes.

Some cities have been easier for the family to live in than others. After adopting all the boys in California, Greg accepted a position with a church in Grand Rapids. With some trepidation, Stillman agreed to move back to his home state, despite his memories of intolerance and homophobia. The best thing about the move, Stillman says, was that it showed the children that they could all move together as a family. To the boys, moving to a new home in the past had always meant moving to a new family. But now they were all moving as one.

Stillman worried about the status of their parental rights outside California. But their social worker convinced them not to worry. "Nobody is going to want your kids," she said.

In Michigan, Stillman and Greg never grew accustomed to the stares they got in public. Waiters routinely asked the family what group home they were from. Greg began to confront people at other tables who gawked, loudly saying, "Stop staring at us." At one restaurant, after a family that had been staring at them was replaced by another leering family, Greg said, "I'm glad you're here. You can see the second show."

One day at school, D's third-grade teacher gave him a Bible and told him to take it home for his dads to read.

It wasn't hard for the Stewarts to pack up and leave Grand Rapids after ten months. Greg accepted a position as minister of the UU Fellowship of Northern Nevada in Reno, and the family bought a modest ranch house on several acres of land. As luck would have it, their next-door neighbors were two lesbians who were fostering and adopting children. Greg and Stillman christened their new home the Rainbow Ranch. And they began to take in rescue animals.

At various times, the Stewarts had three horses, a goat, three pigs, thirty chickens, and two dogs. "Greg wanted to rescue everything," says Stillman. "And he thought the kids would take care of them." Stillman did most of the animal work. And he learned how to make soufflé with all those eggs.

Their growing boys had plenty of room to roam. And they thrived in the public elementary Montessori school. But as the boys grew older, the homogeneity of the Nevada population became trying. The African-American population was less than 4 percent. And the family again began to feel the pains of sticking out.

Stillman was drawn to move back to California. He felt more welcome driving just thirty miles west into Truckee, California. Crossing that invisible border, the family experienced more acceptance. Where they might be stared at in Reno, people in Truckee commented on their nice family, Stillman says.

So when Greg got a call to interview at the First Unitarian Universalist Society in San Francisco, he took it, even though it would mean moving the family again. For the first time, the boys could see more same-sex-headed households. And they could be in a city openly accepting of gays and lesbians.

Middle school being middle school, however, the boys have still felt self-conscious at times. Greg would often stay away from school so the boys wouldn't be seen with two dads. One day, a visit from him prompted one of the boy's friends to say, "I thought that other guy was your dad."

High school has been more accepting for Arthur, Jo, and D. And the Stewart home buzzes with teenage visitors and the family's four dogs: Dommer, a chocolate Labrador retriever; Bugsy, a Japanese chin; Fred, a Bassett hound; and Lucky, a golden retriever, the sole female in the household. Perched on a hill in the Bernal Heights neighborhood, their home has one bathroom. It's officially zoned as a two-bedroom, though they have converted the basement into a third bedroom, shared by Jo, D, and Allen.

The family is adept at navigating the tight quarters with the dogs underfoot. The drawback for Stillman and Greg, however, is that because the house is zoned as a two-bedroom, the county won't approve them to adopt another child.

They would like to adopt again. The need for adoptive homes has not abated in the ten years that they have been parents. More than 510,000 children are in foster care in the United States, according to the U.S. Department of Health and Human Services, and more than 120,000 children await adoptions.

The Stewarts are not deterred by the high cost of living in San Francisco. Or their food bills, which creep toward $2,000 a month. Then there are shoes. The two skateboarders in the family can go through their shoes in as little as a month.

Stillman and Greg are concerned about more than the family budget. As long as there are children who need homes, the two dads will be interested in providing for them. They have paid particular attention to keeping siblings together, and they know there is a possibility that, one day, one of the boys might have a sibling who will join them.

But as they wait, a household of four teens and David keeps them hopping. Most of the boys have struggled with learning and behavioral issues, products of being born addicted and having trouble forming early attachments because of living in so many foster homes. "Now that they're older, they do get into trouble," Stillman says. But Greg and Stillman continue to stand by them as parents do.

Even as the older boys begin to spend more time out in the world, they haven't pushed to get their drivers' licenses, and they don't talk about moving away. "They're not interested in growing up fast," says Greg. "We have four teens, and they want to be home. They realize that a lot of what they were hoping for, they have found."

Greg and Stillman have also found what they were hoping for. "This has been a spiritual transformation," says Greg. "Nothing is impossible if you have faith. Faith in God, in the system, and in your children."

Preacher's Sons *(documentary film)*
www.preacherssons.com

"The ghosts of the past remain if something doesn't come in to change the system for ordinary people."

Ending Torture

The fetid conditions of Cambodian prisons were nothing new to Karen Tse. She had walked the dank corridors of many former Khmer Rouge lockups and crouched by the bars of the over-crowded, damp cells to confer with Cambodian prisoners.

But she was still shocked one day in 1995 by the hollowed brown eyes of a twelve-year-old boy who gazed at her through rusting bars. Shirtless and barefoot, he wore only thin, blue draw-string pants.

"Hey. How *are* you?" Karen asked the boy in Khmer.

He responded shyly, "Hi."

"Why are you here?" she asked.

The boy had been arrested by the police for stealing a bicycle. He was beaten and tortured until he confessed. Then he was left to languish in this cell. He had no trial date. No lawyer. No hope of release.

Karen Tse had been in Cambodia for a year, working for the United Nations as a young lawyer helping to rebuild a legal system that had been decimated by the brutal regime of the

Khmer Rouge. She worked with adults and high-profile political prisoners.

But her encounter with this frail boy opened her eyes to a new dimension of the prisoner problem. Who would advocate for this unknown twelve-year-old? With all the human rights organizations seeking to protect noteworthy defendants, who was safeguarding the rights of the invisible multitude of ordinary people with no access to lawyers and no knowledge of their rights?

Some answers came immediately to Karen's mind from her days at UCLA law school and from her work as a lawyer with the UN. But she knew that she needed more than legal answers to her questions. "I began to realize that the answers weren't about the law. It was also about the spirit," says Karen. "If we're really going to create a worldwide human rights revolution, it's about the spirit."

Karen took a break from her international civil rights work to attend Harvard Divinity School. She had been deferring admission to HDS for a decade, choosing to attend law school first and work in the trenches as a public defender. In 1997, she sensed that the time was finally right to combine her passion for reforming criminal justice practices with her interest in deeper spiritual questions. After graduation from HDS in 2000, she began to envision an organization that could help ordinary citizens who are subjected to torture. She began to build a human rights organization called International Bridges to Justice (IBJ).

A petite, energetic woman in her mid-forties, Karen speaks quickly, her mind so full of ideas, they tumble out in rapid succession. She launched IBJ in 2000, with grand dreams and little money. Her husband, Alexander Wong, a director of the World Economic Forum, was based in Geneva, Switzerland, and she saw that neutral European city, known as a center of diplomacy, as an ideal home for IBJ. In its first ten years, IBJ has trained thousands of public defenders and police officers in Cambodia and China. And it has expanded to Vietnam, Burundi, West Bengal, India, Zimbabwe, and Rwanda to train law enforcement officers and lawyers, and to educate citizens and prisoners about their rights.

"Our mission is to end state-sponsored torture in the twenty-first century and secure due process rights for all," Karen says. "We think it is completely doable."

As lofty as Karen's goals sound, people who have observed her work don't doubt her chances of success. "Her persuasive powers are amazing," says Francis J. James, senior justice advisor at the UN's integrated peace-building mission in Bujumbura, Burundi, and a member of the IBJ board. "I always say, don't bet against her. You'll lose."

Karen and IBJ are "astonishingly effective in China," says Aryeh Neier, president of the Open Society Institute of the Soros Foundation and former executive director of Human Rights Watch. "She has generated immense enthusiasm among the Chinese lawyers who are exposed to IBJ's work."

Having traveled throughout China, Cambodia, and Vietnam, Karen acknowledges that tremendous strides have been made in those countries, as well as around the world, in adopting laws that forbid torturing criminal defendants. What is missing is the implementation and enforcement of those laws. Karen describes IBJ as a "practical, nuts-and-bolts organization that seeks to build communities of conscience with lawyers, engineers, computer consultants, and others who can partner to build legal aid and defender systems throughout the world."

Torture continues to flourish, Karen says, because it is the cheapest form of criminal investigation. The key to ending it, she believes, is to create public defender systems and train police officers and investigators in more effective and humane techniques. "There's a critical link between torture and the absence of defense counsel," says Karen.

She envisions squadrons of defenders spread out across troubled regions of the world. With her characteristic unflagging optimism, Karen says, "We'll go region by region. Country by country."

Karen cannot remember a time in her life when the issue of torture did not plague her. As a young girl, growing up in Los Angeles' Chinatown, she encountered people from many walks of life, including refugees, who spoke of persecution and fleeing their homelands. She had nightmares about brutal prison beatings. "I would wake up suddenly and be deeply disturbed," Karen recalls. "At first I would be relieved that it was just a bad dream. But I knew that at the moment, my nightmare was someone else's reality. I've always had an obsession with ending torture."

Her family attended a Chinese Catholic church, where the Irish priest spoke English and most of the parishioners spoke only Chinese. The congregants were a mix of Buddhists, Taoists, and Confucianists. "Basically, what we saw was community," says Karen. "I grew up with a sense that religion was very fluid."

As an undergraduate student at Scripps College in Claremont, California, she wrote letters to foreign governments demanding fair trials for dissidents around the world. After graduation, she worked at refugee camps in Hong Kong and Thailand, and applied to both law school and divinity school. As a newly minted lawyer in 1990, she worked as a public defender in San Francisco before heading to Cambodia. When she arrived in 1994, there were just a handful of attorneys in a country of thirteen million. "The Khmer Rouge had killed all the attorneys," Karen says. "There were still women in jail for crimes their husbands had committed ten years earlier." Her first project in Cambodia was to train public defenders. The twenty-five public defenders that emerged from that program were the first in the nation's history.

Karen was sometimes worn down by the fierce resistance she encountered when training people about basic human rights. She sought the advice of a nun, Sister Rose, at an orphanage where Karen volunteered each Sunday. Karen saw Sister Rose as an example of simplicity, purity, and love. Rose urged Karen to look for the Christ or the Buddha in each person, even in those who doubted or resisted her.

Sister Rose's words have guided Karen's work ever since. "She really believed in the transformative power of love. She showed me that to really change the world, it's about love and hope and faith. You can't change the world if you don't have faith." That faith doesn't have to be in a supreme being, but it does have to be a faith in people and their ability to transform.

Karen began to pay closer attention to her urge to attend seminary. "I had a deep sense that I had to go to divinity school, but I didn't know why," Karen said. "I knew that to integrate my life and my work, I had to go."

Karen didn't go to divinity school to become a Unitarian Universalist minister. She didn't even know what Unitarian Universalism was until her first year at HDS. During a class on UU polity, or organization, Karen realized—without ever having attended a UU service—that she herself was a Unitarian Universalist. The feeling was confirmed when she started attending—and conducting —UU services during her two-year internship at the Unitarian Universalist Church in Haverhill, Massachusetts. The church also ordained her, cementing Karen's deep love for parish ministry. She harbors a desire to one day be a parish minister, but she also feels an abiding call to train public defenders and end torture.

"First and foremost, I am a spiritual being," says Karen, and IBJ is her ministry. "The legal frameworks are the tools by which we work. But it's really the spirit that moves us. It's the understanding of the interconnectedness and our inherent worth and dignity that really builds the foundations of our work. I couldn't do this without being a lawyer, and I wouldn't have started it without being a minister. Being a minister creates the possibilities of hope and faith."

As Karen imagined what IBJ could be, she consulted another lawyer and Unitarian Universalist minister, Rev. Scotty McLennan, the dean of religious life for Stanford University. He joined the advisory board of IBJ. "Karen has an open vision that goes beyond Christianity," says McLennan. "The core of her vision is that she is serving the whole person, not just the person who happens to be tortured or detained or deprived of basic legal rights, but also the larger issues of social justice and society as a whole. In addition, she has the religious urge to see all of us in the image of God and therefore sacred."

Karen created IBJ in 2000 with more will than money. She decided that China was the place to begin addressing defendants' rights, despite having been there only on tourist trips and knowing little of substance about the country. She had one contact—a Chinese university professor who helped her arrange an appointment with the chief of China's legal aid program. Karen scraped money together to fly to China and borrowed a friend's business suit to look presentable for her appointment. She arrived in China only to find that her one appointment had been cancelled.

But Karen would not take no for an answer. She insisted on a fifteen-minute meeting with the official the next day. With her foot in the door, Karen made her pitch to begin training Chinese defenders. The official assented, and based on that initial meeting, agreed to let her begin to train lawyers and educate prisoners and citizens about their rights. He laid down one condition, however. He told Karen that she must supply four hundred personal computers for legal aid offices. Karen said that it was a deal. Then she had to figure out how her one-person human rights organization could fulfill that promise.

She scrambled to network with friends. Some threw a Hong Kong fundraiser that attracted an anonymous $25,000 donation. At the same time, she became a fellow with Echoing Green, a foundation based in New York that provides seed money and support to young social entrepreneurs. Another friend introduced her to an officer with the George Soros Open Society Institute. The philanthropic organization granted $300,000 to the fledgling IBJ. Emboldened by her success, Karen began to schmooze with more potential donors and received a $5,000 donation from computer industry mogul Michael Dell.

Now she could make her move into China. Working closely with the Ministry of Justice, IBJ has helped to organize training conferences for more than a thousand defenders and distributed more than half a million posters and brochures that promote legal rights in Mandarin, as well as in other regional languages, such as Tibetan, Mongolian, and Uyghur. It has conducted rights-awareness campaigns aimed at both adults and juveniles across thirty-one provinces; created a how-to manual for pubic defenders and a website for local legal aid centers and lawyers; and organized roundtable discussions that bring together police, defenders, prosecutors, and judges to promote cooperation.

In recent years, IBJ has focused on juvenile justice issues in China. In collaboration with the All-China Lawyers Association and Peking University School of Law, IBJ developed a rights-awareness brochure for juvenile suspects titled "A Handbook for Juveniles: What You Should Know if You Are Accused of a Crime." Nearly four thousand copies have been distributed.

IBJ has conducted similar operations in Cambodia and Vietnam, training defenders and educating citizens about the rights guaranteed by their countries' constitutions.

In Cambodia, a former police officer who used to order his subordinates to torture confessions out of defendants is now an IBJ fellow who trains police officers not to torture. Such transformations convince Karen that change is possible on a world scale, as long as people work with individuals to tap into their deeper values. "The ghosts of the past remain if something doesn't come in to change the system for ordinary people," she says. "Unless someone comes in with a new vision, torture will continue for generations to come."

On the heels of her success in Asia, Karen traveled to Africa in 2006 to begin developing a human rights campaign on that continent by meeting with officials in Burundi, Rwanda, and Zimbabwe. She launched her first African project in Burundi, where IBJ has helped to create and distribute posters in both French and Kirundi that read, "You have the right to a defense lawyer, the right not to be tortured, and the right to a fair trial."

IBJ has grown to include twenty-one employees, with an annual budget of $1.8 million. In addition to its Geneva headquarters, it has three offices in China, as well as branches in Burundi, Cambodia, India, Rwanda, Singapore, and Zimbabwe. Karen is based in Geneva, where she lives with her husband and two young sons.

She regularly receives inquiries from countries around the world seeking help in bolstering their human rights work. She's hopeful IBJ can eventually grow to meet the demand. She has set her sites on having 108 trained fellows around the world—who can in turn train more defenders.

The number 108 has great significance for Karen. She subscribes to the theory in Malcolm Gladwell's book *The Tipping Point* that an idea reaches critical mass when 100 people are talking about it. Add to that the number 8, which is the lucky number for Chinese. There are also 108 beads on the Tibetan prayer mala, and a Chinese folktale tells of 108 heroes who saved their country.

Karen was not all at surprised when IBJ staffers conducted a risk assessment to evaluate the number of countries where they could have an impact: 108. "There's wisdom, and there's intuition, and there's the intellectual," says Karen. "108 is just right."

In 2006, Karen and IBJ launched a new program called Communities of Conscience to help involve more volunteers in more countries. It is a cultural exchange program that brings legal-aid lawyers from the developing world to meet with lawyers in North America or Europe for intensive two-week training programs. The lawyers attend trials and visit public defender and legal-aid offices and detention centers. And they develop mentoring relationships with Western lawyers and legal experts.

The first Communities of Conscience exchange brought Chinese lawyers to visit with their counterparts in Dublin, Ireland. The second brought Chinese lawyers to Washington DC. It began with Supreme Court Justice Ruth Bader Ginsburg hosting the defenders at the U.S. Supreme Court.

To help further spread information about defendants' rights and spark reform, IBJ established a JusticeMakers program in 2008. It is an online community that shares intellectual capital and best practices in criminal justice. And it hosts an annual competition to award JusticeMakers grants. IBJ awards the fellowships to people who propose the most novel methods of collaborating with police, legal aid societies, and governments to ensure legal counsel.

Winners receive $5,000 in seed money to implement their innovative criminal justice programs.

JusticeMakers fellows have addressed a wide range of legal issues across the world. In Nigeria, Patrick Dunkwu created a program to help provide legal counsel for indigent criminal defendants by using mobile phones to link lawyers and paralegals with the recently arrested. In Pakistan, Maliq Tahir Iqbal is working to reform the juvenile justice system by addressing the physical and psychological abuse that youth suffer while in detention. And in the Philippines, Rommel Abitria is working to train inmates to become paralegals in an attempt to alleviate problems caused by slow trials, prison congestion, and a lack of inmate training programs.

In 2010, IBJ received 112 applications for JusticeMakers fellowships. The 11 winners hailed from Azerbaijan, Bangladesh, Georgia, India, Indonesia, Malaysia, Pakistan, the Philippines, Sri Lanka, and Vietnam. With her fellowship, H. M. Harshi Chitrangi Perera will provide legal aid for female pretrial detainees in the Women's Ward of the Welikda Prison in Sri Lanka. In her successful application, Chitrangi wrote:

> Overcrowding of prisons leads to torture and cruel, inhuman, degrading treatment and punishment in detention centres in Sri Lanka. The circumstances of the women inmates are at the worst, for the Sri Lanka prisons system is not sensitive to gender. The head of the Women's Ward is a male official.
>
> Inmates face not only instances of actual physical or mental torture, but are subjected to substandard and dehumanizing living conditions like appalling sleeping conditions, lack of basic necessities such as proper sanitation, food, medical attention, shortage of trained officers.
>
> It is also a fact that those being subject to this treatment are those who cannot afford a lawyer to get out of prison or bribes to get preferen[tial] treatment inside prisons. As

such the poor, the marginalized, often become easy targets for torture. . . . Torture prevails despite Sri Lanka ratifying a number of international conventions aimed at preventing torture and ill-treatment.

The JusticeMakers fellowships have allowed IBJ's mission to have a ripple effect across the world. And Karen hopes that IBJ can continue to empower defenders to create waves of reform by establishing innovative programs in their home countries.

As her work has spread, Karen has begun to garner accolades. She was the recipient of the 2008 Harvard Divinity School's First Decade Award, and the 2008 American Bar Association's International Human Rights Award. She also received the 2009 Gleitsman International Award at the Harvard Kennedy School of Government. She remains humble about her accomplishments, however, and cognizant of how much remains to be done to create more bridges to justice.

"People think human rights work has to be about the extraordinary," Karen says. "But it's really the ordinary daily grunt work that ends up making a tremendous difference. If we can inspire ordinary people to do extraordinary things, the world will change."

The twelve-year-old Cambodian prisoner inspired Karen, and it's often memories of a four-year-old boy that sustain her. Karen describes the young Cambodian, Vishna, as her favorite hero. Born in a prison, he had spent his entire life there. He was small enough to slip through the bars. "When I met him, though, he was getting older and could no longer get through the bottom rungs of the prison bars," Karen recalls. "But he could climb up to the third bar, which was slightly bigger, then slowly turn his head to the side and then find a way to barely pass through the bars to the other side."

Every day when Karen arrived, Vishna would take her by the hand and lead her to each prison cell. At each of the 156 cells, he would reach out a hand or a finger to the prisoner inside.

"I often think of Vishna," Karen says. "A boy born into a prison without material or physical comfort. But a boy who had a sense of his own heroic journey and desire to give up a piece of his life to something greater than himself. I think of the contributions he made to the prisoners' wretched lives, both on an individual level as he reached out his hand so many times, and also of the contributions he made to human rights through me, for he so often gave me strength when I was not sure why I should continue on. This heroic spirit and journey to reach behind the bars of injustice is open to all of us."

International Bridges to Justice
www.ibj.org

"I've never met a kid who was beyond help or beyond hope."

Helping Homeless Boys in Guatemala

A story in a magazine changed George Leger's life.

On a Sunday morning in 1993, George had found an open door leading into the empty halls of Central Junior High School in Waltham, Massachusetts. Roaming the corridors of his now-abandoned school, he distantly remembered his early and unhappy teenage years, and he felt empty inside.

Leaving the cavernous, empty building, he eyed the flagpole on the school's front lawn. He sat down against it on the warm May afternoon, facing a whitewashed clapboard church across the street. He opened the Sunday paper, pulled out *The Boston Globe Magazine*, and began to read.

The cover article pulled him in. "Giovanni's Story" detailed the short life and gruesome death of a Guatemalan boy. He had fled his abusive family to live on the streets of Guatemala City. George was riveted and horrified by what he read. Halfway through the article, he closed the magazine and said to himself, "George. You can leave this magazine closed and return to your life as it is. But if you finish it, your life will change forever."

51

George didn't know how it would change. But he knew he would be unable to return to the security and simplicity of his existence as a country-club pastry chef. He paused for several minutes, staring at the church across the street. Then he opened the magazine to where he had left off and read on. Like many of the homeless boys Giovanni lived with, he had been arrested by the Guatemala City police. They beat the boy, tortured him, and abandoned his body in a field on the outskirts of the city. George finished the article, and his life changed forever.

The change began with a retreat into his apartment. George reported for work, but he came home each day, obsessed with thoughts of Giovanni. How is it possible, he wondered, that millions of the world's children were living in the streets? He began to read more about Guatemala and how civil war and poverty had created thousands of homeless children. He read Giovanni's story over and over. "The story dealt a severe blow to my faith in humanity," George says. "More importantly, I would have lost faith in my own humanity if knowing what I knew after reading Giovanni's story, I didn't try to do something about it."

George tracked down the author of the article, Sara Terry, to learn more. He picked her brain about traveling to Guatemala City, and began to plan a trip.

Ten months after reading Giovanni's story, George arrived in Guatemala City. Terry had put him in touch with Childhope, a nonprofit group that provided food and shelter to needy children. Two volunteers from Childhope's Guatemala City office showed George around the streets. They told the kids that George could be trusted, and the kids let him into their world.

George remembers his first night on the city streets as electric. He went to Concordia Park, where the street kids gathered—and where Giovanni had hung out. Children darted about in the dark, and they gathered in groups, laughing and telling jokes.

Half of Guatemala's fourteen million inhabitants are less than eighteen years old. It's estimated that 60 percent of the youth live in poverty and that Guatemala City alone may have as many as five thousand homeless children.

For ten days, the couple from Childhope introduced George to street kids and helped translate their conversations. George left Guatemala City with a vow to return. "I knew I needed to do something just because the need existed," he says. "I feared a lot of people wouldn't understand my need to do it or that they would mock me. But I didn't care. I knew I was in the right place. It was a turning point in my life."

Flying back to Massachusetts, George looked out the window of the plane, flooded with memories of home. He remembered walking through the halls of his junior high school. And he reflected on his teenage years, a time of isolation and great conflict with his father. He was thirty-six years old, but the pain of his teenage years still scarred him. He was haunted by the feeling he'd had as a boy that if he had vanished off the face of the earth, no one would have noticed. George stared into the waters of the Gulf of Mexico and felt like an unspoken prayer had been answered to salve the wounds of his past. A feeling washed over him that if he could help those boys in Guatemala, he could heal himself too.

Back in Massachusetts, the country club where George worked was scaling back its operations to renovate. He negotiated a leave of absence while the club was under construction and began planning his return to Central America. He enrolled in a local adult education class to learn to speak Spanish. And he reached out to friends and family for small donations to help the homeless kids he was going back to see.

If "Giovanni's Story" began the change in George's life, the second trip to Guatamala sealed the transformation. This time, he planned a three-month visit. The city's Childhope office wasn't functioning as well as George had hoped, so he began to connect directly with the children, rather than working through the organization's volunteers.

Each morning, George went to Concordia Park. He's a trim man, with close-cropped brown hair and gentle brown eyes. His short stature put him eye to eye with many of the teenage boys he met in the park. He listened to their stories and talked to the boys, giving the adult time and attention they hungered for. He also met an El Salvadoran woman named Clara, who ran a food stall with her husband Luis on the edge of the park and had been looking out for the boys for several years. George used the bulk of the money he had collected back home to buy breakfast for the boys in the park each day from Clara. Then he hung out with them, playing soccer and talking for the rest of the day.

One day, as he walked through the streets of the city, trying to decide whether to return to Boston, George saw a crowd gathered around a storefront. As he pushed closer, he saw that people were watching a World Cup soccer game on television through the window. To his surprise, the team on TV was playing in Foxboro Stadium, not far from his home in Massachusetts. That flash from home confirmed for George that he didn't want to return. He knew he wanted to stay and help the street kids. And he realized that he needed to start his own nonprofit.

In his Guatemala City apartment, George made a list of twelve people he thought he could count on to pledge as sponsors of a new organization. He asked for just $20 per month from each of them. That would pay for one meal a day for a group of boys and their medical care. And it would allow him to continue to give them time and attention. George launched his new organization in 1994, calling it Only a Child.

Since the mid-1990s, Only a Child has grown from its simple origins of providing a meal and medicine. George opened a group home for the boys. A few years later, he started a carpentry shop, where they could learn a trade, earn money, and contribute to the surrogate family he created. The boys attend school and grow up, looking out for one another. "They must contribute time and effort daily toward meeting the needs of the family," George says. "In return, it gives them something to belong to, a place where they are respected and cared for, a place where they can grow and develop an identity complete with confidence and self-esteem."

The children of Guatemala become homeless for many reasons. A thirty-six-year civil war ended in Guatemala in 1996, leaving the country internally and economically fractured. Many children run away from severely impoverished homes, where they are physically and sexually abused, and many parents suffer from drug and alcohol addiction. Their difficult home lives make the streets look like a better alternative, even for those as young as seven or eight. To survive, the homeless children beg, scavenge, and steal. George was surprised the find that the Guatemalan government did not reach out to help these children. Instead, like Giovanni, they were routinely victims of police beatings and sexual exploitation. The killing of street children became known as "social cleansing."

When he started Only a Child in 1994, the project was simple: to provide the street kids with meals, medicine, and adult companionship. George formed and sponsored four soccer teams for groups of boys. The soccer program was short-lived, however. Fields were frequently closed. And many of the street kids were also battling drug problems and couldn't compete with their healthier peers. Glue sniffing is rampant among the street children. And in the late 1990s, crack cocaine and marijuana became readily available too.

George knew that to really get the kids off the streets, he would have to open a shelter. In 2000, Only a Child bought a house that could accommodate eight boys. Clara and Luis, the couple who ran the restaurant off Concordia Park, moved in to become house parents and cook for the kids.

"We tried to create a family environment," says George. That was no small task for these kids, most of whom had never been exposed to a positive family environment. The house rules were firm. Kids could continue to live there as long as they were attending school.

In 2006, George moved the shelter to a larger building in a residential neighborhood that could accommodate up to twelve youth. It has a dining room that seats twenty, and a large living room where the kids can gather and watch TV. There's a kitchen, a pantry, and a patio with a sink for washing clothes. Each of the three large bedrooms has two sets of bunk beds. George lives in a small apartment a few blocks away. Clara and Luis have since moved on, but he always retains a couple who can live with and cook for the boys.

The boys go to school during the day. The evenings are family time. George talks with the boys, and they play Parcheesi, ping-pong, and foosball. They eat family dinners, and they celebrate each other's birthdays with cake and ice cream and piñatas.

Carlos has been with Only a Child almost since its beginning. George remembers him as a "die-hard street kid" with a "fierce drug addiction."

George met Carlos on the street and saw him in prison, where George used to go each week to check on kids he knew through his outreach program. Carlos had suffered a severe beating, and he told Leger that he was desperate to change his life. Carlos knew that if he didn't get a job, he would fall back into his old ways.

That night, George decided that he had to find a way to offer work to the kids. He had befriended a man named Gregorio who ran a carpentry shop, and he talked to him about teaching the kids carpentry skills.

In addition to a home, food, and school, George knew the boys also needed a skill and a productive way to spend their time. He thought that by learning carpentry, they could begin to feel good about themselves and to contribute to their Only a Child family.

In 2001, George opened a carpentry shop near the shelter. In the shop, the boys learn to craft finely carved cedar boxes that come in a variety of sizes and designs—birds, dolphins, turtles, shells, stars, moons, and hearts. Only a Child sells them for $24 each. The goal is not to turn a profit, but to fund the running of the carpentry shop.

"As they learn to produce a beautifully crafted product, they come to see that when given opportunity, training, and the proper resources, they are indeed capable of accomplishing good and great things, just like anyone else," says George. "Our carpentry shop gives our youngsters the chance to begin to see themselves in a more positive light."

The kids now run the shop in its entirety. George supplies them with the materials, and the boys manage the shop and carve the boxes—more than six hundred each year. "It never occurred to me that they couldn't produce that quality of work," George says. The quality is so high, he says, that he tells the children that they're not just carpenters, they are artisans. "A lot of people enable street kids to remain stuck. But I never condescend to them, and I never allow them to indulge in the 'poor me's.' Only a Child challenges our youngsters to challenge themselves—something that is rare in the life of someone who has grown up in the street."

Gregorio was the shop's original foreman, and Carlos was the second boy to work with him. They worked together for several years, until Gregorio suffered a stroke.

Carlos is now foreman. He lives with his partner, Alicia, and their four children in the Only a Child shelter. Alicia cooks for the boys, and Carlos is their mentor.

Carlos has a natural ability to work with wood, and George has seen him become a father figure to the younger boys. "Only someone in Carlos's position, who was on the streets and suffered on the streets and struggled to get off the streets, can understand the struggle the youngsters coming into the program today have," says George.

Carlos is joined in the shop by a man named Alfredo, who also directs outreach for Only a Child. Alfredo and George teach the boys work habits and how to be good employees. "Growing up on the street in no way prepares them to be honest and productive workers. That's the main focus of the shop. And as we teach them to be good, honest, valuable employees, they're also developing good character."

Since the shelter opened, fifty kids have lived there. And George counts more than half of them as success stories, meaning that they have attained some degree of self-sufficiency and have not returned to living on the streets. He mentors and guides them, and he sets high expectations. "The kids end up thanking me for being tough on them," he says.

George has lived in Guatemala for more than fifteen years. He still flies back to Boston a few times a year to touch base with family and friends, and to fundraise.

He established Only a Child as a nonprofit in the United States so he can solicit tax-deductible donations from American donors. Individual gifts comprise about 60 percent of Only a Child's annual budget. George also relies on grants, fundraisers, and gifts from members of his Boston church community, the Arlington Street Church, a Unitarian Universalist church in downtown Boston.

The Arlington Street Church encourages its members to donate to causes that advance human rights and social, economic, and environmental justice. It lists Only a Child as one of the organizations to support. George visits the church when he returns to the United States and maintains close ties with his donors and friends there. George, who was raised Catholic, says that he has returned to his Christian roots and that he tries to follow the teachings of Jesus. He frequently quotes the Bible in his fundraising newsletters. He addresses those newsletters, "To the many who have cared." And he invokes Jesus' words found in the Gospel According to Matthew: "For I was hungry and you gave me food, I was thirsty and you gave me something to drink, I was a stranger and you welcomed me, I was naked and you gave me clothing, I was sick and you took care of me, I was in prison and you visited me. . . . Truly I tell you, just as you did it to one of the least of these who are members of my family, you did it to me." (Matt. 25: 35–36, 40).

George is also drawn to Unitarian Universalism and the many positive relationships he has formed within that tradition. He embraces the Unitarian Universalist ideas of religious tolerance and its value of being of service to others.

When he recalls the day in 1993 when he read Giovanni's story, leaning against a flagpole outside his old school, he remembers staring at a white church across the street as he decided whether to keep reading the story that would become so pivotal. It was a Unitarian Universalist church, First Parish in Waltham.

When he stared at the church, deciding what step to take next, George could not have anticipated that he would move to Guatemala and reshape the lives of boys who could have ended up like Giovanni. Had he known, he might not have been able to take the next simple steps in his journey toward helping those children.

"I have found that most important work begins with something small or modest, and with time, if the conditions are right, it may lead to something greater," he says. So much of his time in Guatemala is spent fulfilling perfectly mundane tasks—grocery shopping with the boys on Saturdays and joking and playing games with what he describes as a rather large, unorthodox group of children and youngsters.

One of the great challenges for him on a daily basis is "to find joy in the most ordinary tasks, make peace with the more difficult ones, and complete both with as much love as possible." George says it's easy to understand but not always easy to put into practice. But it is his daily meditation.

He's aided by his deep faith in and hope for the children. He has a bottomless belief in their ability to pull themselves back from the life of addiction and homelessness to become educated, productive members of society with a sense of their own self-worth. "I look at these kids, and realize that I've never met a kid who was beyond help or beyond hope," he says.

George also has limitless hope in other people to make a difference in the lives of those in need. "We all have the potential to make a difference," he says. "What each individual should try to remember is that they're not working alone. There are billions of others who can work with them. All they need to do is their part."

Only a Child
www.onlyachild.org

"When I reflect on my life, being a part of the startup of Jericho Road is one of the high points."

Revitalizing Struggling Cities

Dozens of women in wedding gowns are crossing an iron bridge over the Merrimack River on a September afternoon. Alongside men in dark suits, they file past the abandoned brick mill buildings that line the streets of Lawrence, Massachusetts. Children dart among them, carrying signs: "Real Men Don't Batter," "You Do Not Deserve to Be Abused," and "*Amor Es Libertad*" ("Love Is Freedom").

The Brides' March commemorates Gladys Ricart, a Dominican-American woman who was fatally shot on her wedding day by her former boyfriend. The walk marks the tenth anniversary of that New Jersey killing, honoring Ricart as well as the thirty-one Massachusetts residents who have died from domestic violence in the first three-quarters of 2009. Although the annual march once attracted primarily Dominican women, each year it has become more interracial. A state representative and a mayoral candidate have joined the walk, as has Miss Massachusetts.

At the head of the somber line of people in white dresses and black clothes walks Mary McAlary in a tailored white suit, wide-brimmed hat, pearls, and running shoes. McAlary is the president of Delamano, a Lawrence-based nonprofit that provides victims of domestic violence a Spanish and English helpline and access to emergency services. Delamano is the only helpline available to domestic violence victims in the city after 5 P.M. But after its state funding was cut, McAlary says, they have been "living hand to mouth." Much of their survival she credits to a dedicated group of Unitarian Universalist volunteers who have come to her through an organization called the Jericho Road Project. "We'd never be in the position we are in today if it weren't for the help of Jericho Road," says McAlary.

The Jericho Road Project—affiliated with several Unitarian Universalist congregations—matches white-collar volunteers who can donate professional services to nonprofit organizations in need of help with specific projects. Jericho Road volunteers have assisted Delamano with budgeting, computer networking, graphic design, web design, and insurance. Husband and wife Dave Kovner and Donna Cloney volunteer their professional expertise in public relations and marketing work to publicize the Brides' March. Their publicity has attracted TV crews and reporters from the local English and bilingual newspapers.

Kovner and Cloney are members of North Parish Unitarian Universalist Church in the adjacent town of North Andover. They have come to the walk with seven other church members, who also belong to Cloney's small group ministry. In a full-length wedding gown with puffy lace sleeves, Cloney hands out fliers to curious onlookers as the parade of brides snakes towards city hall, drawing spectators out of storefront markets and beauty parlors.

Delamano is one of about a hundred nonprofit organizations in the Merrimack Valley to receive assistance from the Jericho Road Project. The project was created in 2003 by a group of members of the First Parish in Concord that included venture capitalists, bankers, and consultants who were trying to create a new model of social justice work. Situated on a wide green in the center of Concord—historic home of Ralph Waldo Emerson, Henry David Thoreau, and Louisa May Alcott—the church had traditionally focused its social justice efforts on charity work, but these members were interested in finding hands-on opportunities to create more systemic change. The Concord group has concentrated its efforts on serving nonprofits in Lowell, a once prosperous city of textile mills twenty-five miles north of the affluent Boston suburb. Lowell and Concord sit on opposite ends of the demographic spectrum. The median household income in Lowell hovers just below $40,000. Violent crime and property crime are the fourth highest in the state. In Concord the median household income is more than $115,000. Sprawling Colonials on manicured lawns routinely sell for more than $1 million.

The North Andover church started its chapter of Jericho Road two years later in 2005, and has concentrated on Lawrence, which, like Lowell, has suffered as manufacturing jobs have disappeared. "We're focused on helping small, poor, post-industrial cities," says Dan Holin, executive director of the project.

Jericho Road seeks to help these cities and their residents by aiding established nonprofit organizations there. The project supplies management consultants, lawyers, bankers, executive coaches, software designers, and other professionals who can work with them on specific projects. "The nonprofits are on the front line in the community," says First Parish minister Rev. Jenny Rankin. "We're trying to help them become stronger."

The success of Jericho Road in Lowell and Lawrence has spurred other UU churches and organizations to replicate their work. New Jericho Road organizations have been established in two other Massachusetts cities and in Pasadena, California. The work is complex, but the process is straightforward. "We're matchmakers," says Holin, pairing white-collar volunteers with nonprofits. The goal: to enhance the quality of life by building the capacity of nonprofits through skills-based volunteering. In the process, Holin says, they enrich the lives of the volunteers too.

A sermon by Rev. Martin Luther King Jr. inspired the name for the Jericho Road Project. In his controversial 1967 address "Beyond

Vietnam," King spoke of a "true revolution in values" that would call people to "question the fairness and justice of many of our past and present policies." He said,

> On the one hand, we are called to play the Good Samaritan on life's roadside, but that will be only an initial act. One day we must come to see that the whole Jericho Road must be transformed so that men and women will not be constantly beaten and robbed as they make their journey on life's highway. True compassion is more than flinging a coin to a beggar. It comes to see that an edifice which produces beggars needs restructuring.

Rankin suggested the name Jericho Road to a group of First Parish members who had come together to form a new outlet for social action at the church. She assembled the group in 2000, after hearing a repeated refrain from members that they did not feel as if the church's social action programs tapped their talents. At the same time, people wanted to engage in social action that created systemic change rather than charity work that felt like "flinging coins to beggars."

"We talked a lot about the concept of teaching people to fish rather than providing fishes," says Tony Gallo, one of a dozen First Parish members in the original brainstorming sessions. After a few years of discussions, a concept began to emerge. First Parish formed a nonprofit organization independent from the church, selected a board of directors, and hired Dan Holin as executive director.

Holin had recently relocated to Concord from Israel. He had worked for a year for the Massachusetts Cultural Council, building bridges between museums and minority communities. The Jericho Road job was also about building bridges, he recalls. "My whole life has been bridging," says Holin. The son of an American mother and an Israeli father, Holin grew up in both countries. He wasn't familiar with churches, Concord, or Lowell, but Jericho Road intrigued him.

He began to try to make inroads into Lowell, with little sense of whether he could succeed. "It was like running around in the woods, trying to find a way out," he says. Holin launched a small marketing campaign to Lowell nonprofit groups to promote Jericho Road volunteers. To his surprise, his first request came from the largest social service agency in Lowell, Community Teamwork Inc. (CTI), which needed help creating a new strategic plan.

Holin laughs at the memory of the large request of their novice firm. Tall and thin with short brown hair and a graying goatee, he is always quick with a comparison. "It was like a house contractor suddenly being asked to build a skyscraper," he says. But he didn't say no. Two Jericho Road volunteers held two days of public strategic planning meetings in Lowell and delivered a top-notch strategic plan to CTI. "That strategic plan was a credibility builder," Holin says. "The attitude of nonprofits toward Jericho Road turned from mild skepticism to awe."

From that initial project, Jericho Road has become woven into the fabric of the Lowell nonprofit community. Since 2003, it has assisted more than 125 nonprofit organizations. Holin estimates that in 2009 Jericho Road volunteers provided $500,000 of professional help to Lowell nonprofits alone, at a cost of about $100,000. "While it's possible to quantify the dollar value of Jericho Road's services, it is much harder to quantify the value of their impact," says Holin. "A personal coach delivering ten hours of counseling to a distressed nonprofit executive director may be worth $1,000. But if that counseling kept the talented director from leaving the organization, the value of the impact is far greater than the value of the service itself."

Even the $500,000 estimate may be conservative. On the free market, Tony Gallo, a marketing and strategy consultant, commands a rate of $4,000 per day. "Clearly, that is out of reach of these organizations. If I charged $100 a day, that would be too much," says Gallo. His first project with Jericho Road was to help write a speech for a union leader and then coach her in presenting it. He also aided the Lowell Community Health Center in developing a strategic marketing plan.

"It's unbelievable how rewarding the work is," says Gallo, who had never done volunteer work before.

John Conley, another First Parish member and president of the Jericho Road Lowell board of directors since 2008, also finds the work intellectually and spiritually rewarding. "I think of the key arms of my faith as a direct spiritual experience and an active service component. And this is the active service component. It's extremely fulfilling, helping me with an itch that had always been there and hadn't been scratched."

By day, Conley is partner and cofounder of Gilliam Capital, a life-science investment firm in Concord. In his first stint with Jericho Road he advised the Lowell Southeast Asian Water Festival, an annual celebration of the cultures of the thousands of Khmer, Thai, Vietnamese, and Laotian residents in Lowell. Prior to working with Jericho Road, Conley says, he never would have found himself "sitting around a table, trying to solve problems with a second-generation Laotian, and a Cambodian refugee, trying to plan a Buddhist festival." He has worked with people who personally, or through family members, lived through the brutality of the Pol Pot regime or the Vietnam War, and have come to Lowell to find a better life. "If it weren't for Jericho Road, I wouldn't be able to have that experience," he says.

Jodi DeLibertis can't drive very far in Lowell without passing the door of an agency that Jericho Road has helped. The program director of Jericho Road Lowell, DeLibertis spends little time in her office, a desk in a redeveloped yarn factory across the railroad tracks from downtown Lowell. Mostly, she is driving her aging green minivan from one nonprofit to the next. "I have the best job in the world," says DeLibertis. "My daughter says all I do is take people out to coffee. That's about half of it."

She joined Jericho Road in 2007, around the same time she became a member of First Religious Society of Newburyport, Massachusetts. "I find Jericho Road and First Religious Society mutually reinforcing," she says as she points out Jericho Road landmarks.

Out the left window, she indicates a playground under construction that was planned by a volunteer landscape architect. She passes the Senior Center, the Hellenic Center, and the city library, all clients. "There's the Lowell House substance abuse prevention center," she says, for which a graphic designer and communications expert produced a brochure. She ticks off more clients as she drives: a Cambodian dance troupe, a center for Southeast Asian children, a legal services clinic. One brick building houses two clients: the Rape Crisis Services Center of Greater Lowell and the International Institute, which provides immigration and refugee services. She passes the Greater Lowell Community Foundation ("We did their annual report") and the New Entry Sustainable Farming Project ("We helped recruit people for their advisory board"). For the Lowell Telecommunications Corp., Jericho Road volunteers help set up wireless communications downtown.

DeLibertis walks into one of Lowell's great nonprofit success stories, the United Teen Equality Center (UTEC), a teen drop-in center in downtown Lowell aimed at curbing gang violence. Started in 1999 in a church basement, with a $40,000 budget and three volunteer staff members, the center has blossomed into a multifaceted agency now housed in a converted Methodist church. It serves more than a thousand teens each year, with an annual budget of $850,000 and nine full-time staff. UTEC offers a culinary and catering program, a farm program, free after-school mental health counseling, GED programs, social clubs, and political groups. The church's former sanctuary is a basketball court, its stained-glass windows casting multicolored light onto weight rooms where the side aisles used to be.

A Jericho Road volunteer architect helped UTEC staff select and renovate the new space. Other volunteers have helped the center with brand strategy, legal issues, market research, web development, and database management. Another volunteer set up UTEC's phone and computer systems (as he did for Lowell's

Quilt Museum, Revolving Museum, and other nonprofits). Jessica Wilson, UTEC's director of development, has been impressed by the commitment of all the volunteers who give time to UTEC. "Having the ability to work with gangs doesn't mean that we have the expertise with IT or legal issues," she says. "But I can call Jodi for help with these things, and I can work on what we do best."

When Jericho Road Lowell was first established, it concentrated on finding volunteers to meet specific requests from nonprofits. As Holin and DeLibertis have become immersed in the nonprofit community, however, they have started to anticipate needs and identify broader issues that need addressing. "We're also a nonprofit, so we have an eye-level view," says Holin. "Because we know our clients, and they are our colleagues, we build trust and talk with them about what they need."

For example, DeLibertis used to get many requests for graphic design and marketing materials. But talking with volunteers, she began to realize that the clients often did not have a strong enough grasp of marketing issues to know what they needed. So she offered a marketing workshop for nonprofits last year. Forty-five people attended a crash course, learning about market research, branding, and public relations. "Now we're starting to get different kinds of marketing requests," she says, "and our copywriters and graphic designers are getting used better." Similarly, she organized a seminar on nonprofit finance in the fall of 2010.

At Jericho Road Lawrence, Executive Director Joan Kulash heard repeated requests from nonprofits for assistance researching and writing grants. In response, she helped create a grant resource center for nonprofits in the campus library of the Northern Essex Community College, with the aid of Associated Grant Makers. Prior to the center's opening, employees and volunteers at Lawrence nonprofits had to travel thirty miles to Boston to use AGM's free database.

Finding qualified board members is a common concern. As a result, Jericho Road launched the Leadership Connection, a sixteen-hour program to train and place executives from area corporations on nonprofit boards. The program simultaneously generates revenues for Jericho Road and finds community service opportunities for executives.

Like the nonprofits it supports, Jericho Road continually seeks grants to fund its good works. It relies on donations from individual and corporate sponsors, as well as private and public grants. In October 2010, it received its first federal grant, a $150,000 award through the Compassion Capital Fund aimed at organizations that provide social services to low-income communities. In the grant world, money often follows money. So DeLibertis hopes that with one federal grant under their belts, more federal money will follow. "It opens up a new world of opportunity for us," she says.

As the Jericho Road model proves itself in Lowell, other churches have begun to take note and investigate ways to replicate its success. Some are within other UU churches. Some come from other faith and secular communities.

The North Andover church started its Jericho Road Lawrence program after Rev. Lee Bluemel heard Dan Holin describe the Lowell program at a large church conference. "What attracted me to the model is that it appeals to people of all political bents: Green, Democrat, Republican," says Bluemel. She finds that a new sector of the congregation has become involved in social action at the church, including more men than had previously participated in the church's social justice work.

Members of the Unitarian Universalist Church of Reading, Massachusetts, have recently joined the North Andover church in volunteering at Lawrence nonprofits.

In June 2009, a Jericho Road chapter was launched in Worcester, as a partnership between the First Unitarian Church of Worcester and the city's First Baptist Church. In its first year, Jericho Road Worcester initiated twenty-five projects with local nonprofits, including a family farm and the Massachusetts Audubon Society.

A Lynn chapter began in January 2010—the first to spring

from a secular organization. Its volunteers are employees who work at a General Electric facility within the city, and it is run by a partnership with General Electric's Boston Volunteer Council and in collaboration with the Lynn Nonprofit Business Alliance and the Greater Lynn Chamber of Commerce. It provides volunteers to nonprofits in Lynn, which, like Lowell and Lawrence, was once a manufacturing hub that has fallen on hard times since factories began moving south or overseas.

"UU churches are a good launching pad for Jericho Road affiliates," says Holin, but they're not the only one. But he is careful to note that even though Jericho Road chapters most often originate from churches, the program is not a traditional faith-based model. "We're born out of a church, but our values are humanist. People in all kinds of organizations that Jericho Road serves can relate to that," says Holin. "We have no faith agenda, and we don't proselytize."

Jericho Road's first offshoot outside Massachusetts opened its doors in the spring of 2010. Jericho Road Pasadena, in California, was launched from the Neighborhood Unitarian Universalist Church of Pasadena. Prior to its official opening, supporters of the chapter raised enough money to cover the salary of a part-time director, operating costs, and the technical support and expertise of the Jericho Road Project.

Both the Pasadena church (760 members) and the Concord church (nearly 800) are large. A church needs a sizeable membership to generate the number of skilled volunteers to serve a nonprofit community. That's why smaller churches, such as North Andover (370 members) and Worcester (450), have found partner institutions. Holin says that a Jericho Road Project also needs a cluster of urban nonprofits within a thirty-minute drive and a funding community that can support the work.

To support future Jericho Road sites, Holin has developed a "replication manual" and workshops to help new groups get started. Jericho Road Lawrence operates as its own independent nonprofit. The other chapters, in Worcester, Lynn, and Pasadena, are affiliate sites of Jericho Road Lowell, which has grown to four full-time employees and an annual budget of $420,000.

As it investigates opening future sites, the Jericho Road Project will begin to charge local groups for the process of investigating whether it can support a local offshoot. And it will charge a fee for ongoing management of new sites. "It takes up a lot of our time and tools that we've developed over the years," says Holin. "We will need to get paid for our time, our brand, and our knowledge."

Jericho Road is hoping to establish a new site in Boston's Roxbury neighborhood through the Unitarian Universalist Urban Ministry. It is yet another new model for Jericho Road, because it would be run through the structure of an existing nonprofit. Volunteers would come from suburban Boston Unitarian Universalist churches.

Holin has been flexible in adopting different models at different sites. But he's hoping Jericho Road can settle on a workable structure that it can replicate. "You can't grow a business by reinventing every time you take a new step, and that is what we've been doing," he says. "We need to mature and settle down on a model." He's hoping the Urban Ministry model of expanding through existing urban nonprofits will be the method of choice. It would allow Jericho Road to build quickly, rather than having to reinvent investing relationships, funding streams, and office systems at each new urban site. "It may be the future," says Holin. But he quickly adds, "Who knows? We'll see how it goes."

When First Parish in Concord established Jericho Road, all of its volunteers were church members. As word has spread about the group, however, volunteers with no connection to the church have joined from the community at large. Rev. Rankin sees an opportunity. "People hear about Jericho Road, and then they hear about our church," she says. "Then they have a better understanding about what Unitarian Universalism is."

Even with outside volunteers joining Jericho Road in increasing numbers, however, Holin believes that the church and Jericho

Road will always be intrinsically linked. "We are the church's spawn," he says. "And they're in our DNA."

On the last Sunday in October 2009, members of First Parish in Concord have gathered for worship in a service focused on Jericho Road. Katharine Esty, one of the founding board members of Jericho Road, gives the call to worship. She recalls a time, before Jericho Road, when she volunteered with other church members to paint an apartment for a woman with disabilities in low-income housing. Her painting skills were poor, the woman criticized the group for being too messy, and she found herself wishing she could volunteer her strategic planning skills instead.

A few years later, after Jericho Road was established, Esty was able to do just that. "When I reflect on my life," she told the congregation, "being a part of the startup of Jericho Road is one of the high points."

From the pulpit, First Parish's senior minister, Rev. Gary E. Smith, recalled the words of Martin Luther King Jr. from the sermon that gave its name to the Jericho Road Project. Smith told the story of the Good Samaritan, who helped the man who was robbed and beaten on the Jericho Road. "I'd never heard the Jericho Road story in the way King described it," Smith said. "I'd never considered the road itself and what it stood for."

Dan Holin and Jodi DeLibertis looked up from the pews. Founding board members, current board members, and volunteers were there too. And DeLibertis had set up a table at coffee hour—stocked with pastries from a Brazilian bakery in Lowell—to entice new volunteers.

Smith invoked the early Universalists, who ushered in a faith centered on building up a blessed community in the here and now, rather than focusing on an afterlife. Jericho Road's work fits squarely in the tradition, he said, in its concern for others. "Do we love our neighbors as ourselves," he asked, "so our neighbors can be fed and loved and share in the joy of community?"

"The Jericho Road Project is going right at systemic change.

Moving down the Jericho Road is high-risk work for us, because we are the mighty and the rich. But we are also the people who can make change happen. We have the way, if we have the will," Smith preached. "The work of justice remains. We are building a beloved community, and all must be included."

The Jericho Road Project
www.jerichoroadproject.org

"I got a PhD in AIDS mothering. . . . I got it from the professorship of my six children."

Fighting for People with HIV/AIDS

Natalie Bryson and her son David stepped into the cemetery director's car for a tour. They were going to pick out a plot in Seattle's picturesque Lake View Cemetery—one with a nice view of the University of Washington and the Cascade and Olympic mountains.

David sat in front, a breathtakingly handsome model who turned heads everywhere he went. Natalie sat behind the driver, peeking between the front seats in search of the perfect plot.

"That's where Bruce Lee is buried," the driver said, pointing to the gravestone of the martial arts icon. "And that's the mausoleum of the Rhodes family," he narrated, as they passed a large monument dedicated to the Washington department store family, and he indicated that there was a single plot nearby.

David's ears perked up. "That wouldn't be too bad," he said. "Then I know my mother would come to visit me at least once a month, because she never missed the Rhodes end-of-the-month sale."

The driver swung his head around and swerved. "He almost

drove into the Rhodes mausoleum," Natalie says. He had assumed that the plot was for her, an aging mother of six children. But it was for her handsome son.

David was HIV-positive. He died of AIDS in 1994 at thirty-four and was buried in Lake View Cemetery in the plot he picked, close to Bruce Lee. It had a view of his alma mater, the University of Washington. He told his mother that he knew he would always get plenty of visitors with such a famous neighbor.

Three years later, David's brother James, Natalie's youngest child, died of AIDS too. The boys were two years apart in age and had been very close. James and his partner Sean had been David's primary caregivers in his final months. James, who passed away at thirty-five, had lived with his illness for thirteen years before he died, a remarkable amount of time in the early years of the disease.

It is easy to imagine someone with Natalie's losses retreating into solitude or self-pity. But that is not her style. She is an optimist to the end. "My sons helped me through this," she says. "I am so fortunate that I have no unfinished business with either of them. If I am blessed with anything, it is my friends and my family, and particularly my children and my sister, Muriel."

Natalie knows that it can be hard for people, even those who support gay rights, to deal with society's prejudices. Fear of other people's reactions can be an obstacle. "It took three trips to Ohio to visit my sister before I could tell her that the boys were gay and HIV positive," she says. "I should have known, however, that she would not only accept this news but be a great source of strength and support."

Natalie sparkles when she talks. Her hair is a gleaming white. Her lipstick is bright red, her skin is porcelain, and her blue eyes beam. She carries herself with a poise and steeliness forged through years of masking her troubles. "I had to be adorable with such heartache," she says. She has learned to be like bamboo: "strong, open and flexible."

Bryson's unexpected divorce at age fifty-one opened the door to a new career—leading tours to China. Her sons' suffering gave her the incentive and the drive to give back to her community. She resuscitated the then-foundering Kitsap County HIV AIDS Foundation (KCHAF). She became its president and turned it into a powerful local resource. Her mission was to bring the kind of support and services available to people in Seattle across the Puget Sound to her community on the Kitsap Peninsula.

Years later, when the Pride Foundation hosted An Evening Honoring Natalie Bryson to celebrate her contributions and to present her with its inaugural Community Treasure Award, she deflected their praise with characteristic humility and good humor. The revitalization of the HIV/AIDS foundation was "just something that had to get done," she said.

Her friends, neighbors, colleagues, fellow members of the Kitsap Unitarian Universalist Fellowship, and her living children were full of accolades and compliments, calling her an inspiration and a community treasure. Bryson gave the praise right back: "It was what they taught me, not what I taught them," she said. "No one does this alone."

Natalie became an activist because she needed to tell the story of her sons at a time when very few people wanted to talk about homosexuality or AIDS.

In the early 1980s, AIDS and HIV were surrounded by a cloud of silence and shame. Many people viewed AIDS as a "gay disease" inflicted on homosexuals as a punishment from God. Natalie and her sons knew, however, that if people couldn't talk about the disease, they couldn't find a cure either. Knowledge would lead to tolerance, and tolerance would lead to treatment.

David had been living abroad in London and Japan, working as a model. After he became ill and was diagnosed with HIV, he returned to the Pacific Northwest to be closer to family. He became active in Seattle's HIV/AIDS Support Group in the heart of the city's gay community on Capitol Hill. David told his mother that what the center really needed was a way to help the mothers of the men who were infected. He had seen many men struggling with how to tell their mothers they were sick. In many cases, they told their mothers on the same day that they were gay and that they were HIV positive, at a time when the disease had no treatment, and the diagnosis was a death sentence. The mothers needed a place to go to support one another.

Natalie went to the center every Wednesday afternoon and helped start a support group for mothers of people infected with and affected by HIV and AIDS. Mothers began to come from every walk of life—from Seattle's fanciest neighborhoods to its poorest. Some came on the very day their sons shared their tragic news. "We had everything from swearing and yelling and carrying on to shock," recalls Natalie. Whatever the mothers needed to do, they could do it there with others who could understand them and what they were going through.

Many, like Natalie, weren't public about their sons' diagnoses at that time, so having a place where they could be open and honest was essential to their ability to carry on for themselves and to be there for their sons. For the first time in her life, Natalie was working full-time. She couldn't risk being open about her personal struggles at work.

In 1983, when she and her husband of thirty-five years divorced, Bryson needed a job. She assumed she would have to work as a waitress. She had no work experience and no college education. She had her eye on a position at Elsie's Restaurant in Silverdale. But fate had something else in mind.

Natalie had a lifelong interest in China and Chinese porcelain. She studied both avidly and collected what she could. Her hobby spawned a friendship with the director of a museum in Milton, Massachusetts, who oversaw an extensive collection of art and antiquities from the Chinese export trade. The director included Natalie on a trip to the People's Republic of China shortly after Chinese-American relations were normalized, and Americans were allowed to travel there. "It was life-changing," says Bryson. "I had such an affinity for Chinese culture and for the people I met there. It was like I had found a part of myself I didn't know was missing."

When she returned from China, Natalie was invited to give a talk about her trip to a local corporation where many military veterans worked. "My speech had a very bad reception at first," she recalls. "They were a group of Korean War veterans, and they didn't like China and didn't want to know about China." She tossed out her prepared speech and spoke to the men off-the-cuff about what had happened in China since the Korean War. "It was the best speech I ever gave," she says; the men responded with applause.

The following day, Natalie got a call from an executive at a Seattle tourism company who had been struggling to find someone to consult with the company on China issues as it began to plan and lead trips there. Natalie signed on as a consultant that day, and within a year, was working full-time at the company and leading the trips to China herself.

She worked for that company for twenty years, traveled to China twenty-four times, and visited all seven continents. She believes her earlier life had prepared her for it perfectly. Her former husband had been a career naval officer, and the family had moved thirty times in thirty years while she raised six children. "If you move thirty times with six children, you can do anything," Natalie says. She never did apply for the job at Elsie's.

Bryson is a cheerful ambassador for her country and led her trips with charm and grace, even while her sons were ill. She remembers leading a trip for 130 people through the Panama Canal while her heart ached for James, who had recently told her he was HIV positive. "You're never just yourself. You're always the mom," she says. "On one level, I felt totally and completely unable to cope. But you have to learn to cope in order to function." Natalie needed her job to support herself and her sons. So she put on a smile and led her charges through the Panama Canal, along the Great Wall of China, and around the world.

Natalie commuted by ferry across the Puget Sound to her job and to see David in Seattle. James was living in Portland, Oregon.

Although the Seattle AIDS support groups were firmly established, there were few resources in the communities west of Puget Sound, and one of those few, the Kitsap County HIV AIDS Foundation, was struggling. While Seattle had a thriving gay community, a socially conservative tone predominated on the peninsula. Natalie's friend Kathleen Davenport, another supportive mother involved in the community and a KCHAF volunteer, asked Natalie to attend a meeting of the Kitsap group.

Together, Kathleen and Natalie started a Kitsap mothers' group at KCHAF, like the one that had propped them both up in Seattle. Few mothers came, however—many of them fearing to go public about their children's illness. To create a more supportive environment, Natalie and Kathleen decided to shift the focus to offering service to the women's children. Among other initiatives, they started the Red Ribbon Supper Club. Once a month, they provided a home-cooked dinner in a local church for people with HIV and AIDS and their friends and family.

KCHAF was running on a shoestring. Natalie steadily increased her involvement until she was running it from a command center in her dining room. In a grant application to fund the supper club, she described the importance of the monthly gatherings, and how it provided people with a place to connect with one another and their families—and to eat "gooey desserts." Bryson later learned that KCHAF won the funding largely on the merits of her description of the treats at the meal's end.

Bryson also began to share her story publicly to promote tolerance for people with AIDS. She would speak about AIDS wherever she was invited—community groups, conservative churches, anywhere with an audience. And she had a powerful story to tell.

She told people about her son James in Portland, who was a community activist, working to educate youth about HIV and AIDS. He was the western director of the Names Project, which produced the AIDS Memorial Quilt to remember people who have died of the disease. James was instrumental in arranging for the quilt to travel to Washington DC, for a rare full display. President Bill Clinton came out to the National Mall to view it. A personal letter from Clinton to James thanking him is one of Bryson's most prized possessions. Clinton wrote, "The Quilt is an inspiring celebration of the power of love and the enduring strength of the human spirit."

Bryson also told people about her son David, working at the Seattle AIDS Support Group as a drug and alcohol counselor, and as a board member of a charity that provided therapeutic massage to persons with HIV and AIDS. She didn't shy away from naming HIV and AIDS. And she told people how she had learned to let go of society's prejudices and erroneous assumptions about the disease and those who suffer from it.

James was diagnosed with HIV in 1984 when he was twenty-two years old. Natalie frankly admits that her first instinct was to do what she had always done as a mother—take charge. She asked questions and tried to find out as much as she could about James and his disease. Without discussing it with him, she called his doctor and began asking questions about his illness and his prognosis. But his doctor wouldn't answer. He said he couldn't discuss James without his permission, and that he would have to tell her son that she had called.

James was furious with his mother for invading his privacy. She immediately drove four hours down to Portland and spent an emotional weekend with him. They paced on the beach together and cried and yelled and talked. "I was bound and determined that we would have reconciliation; otherwise, I might have never seen him again," Natalie said. By the end of the weekend, they came to an agreement that Natalie would never ask James about his illness and that James would always tell her everything she needed to know. Natalie always kept her word, and James kept his. "I obeyed his rules, and he was sensitive to my needs. Our whole existence was one of great love and thought and consideration, and I don't regret one moment of any of it. It was the most important learning experience of my life."

Natalie took away many lessons. "I learned to get to know people that I never thought I would ever have in life, from hobos to heaven knows. I got to know the gay community and how loving and caring they can be. I learned that just because someone might have been a drug addict or an alcoholic, they could still support me. I learned all kinds of things about life that I never would have known but for these experiences."

Approaching eighty, Natalie still talks to people about AIDS. She tells them what her son James always told her: "Don't give up five minutes before the miracle happens." The miracle that happened to her was learning to accept life as it unfolds. "It wasn't a million dollars or a cure for the boys. It was acceptance," she says.

Her words have helped many. After she spoke at a conservative church, a young mother approached her and said that after seeing her congregation accept Natalie and her story, she thought they might now support her and her struggle with AIDS. A retired military officer told her that he didn't realize that HIV and AIDS could be a problem for elderly people, and that she had opened his eyes to a new dimension of the disease

Others have not been as receptive to Natalie's message. She has lost lifelong friendships because people saw the fact that she had gay sons with AIDS as a moral failing on her part and theirs. She had to overcome the feeling of shame that people tried to put on her. "As James always said, 'You're only as sick as your secrets.' It's important to share the secrets, to bring them into the light," says Natalie. "How people respond to your secrets is up to them."

When David died in October 1994, Natalie submitted his obituary to her local newspaper. An editor called and told her they couldn't print it as it was, because it said that he had died of complications of AIDS, which was against the paper's policy. But Natalie wouldn't be silenced. Instead she bought a tribute advertisement for David and published the obituary in its entirety. "There was a lot of embarrassment in those old days if someone had AIDS," she says. "But the only way you could educate anyone was if they saw that this was a wonderful boy, so handsome and smart, and that he died due to this disease."

By the time his brother James died in September 1997, acceptance had grown. He received a feature story in the obituary section of the *Seattle Times*, which explicitly told readers that he had died of complications of AIDS in his Portland home. The story's lead made James sound like he was his mother's son: "James Hill Bryson had a simple philosophy towards life: 'There's only one thing you really have to do and that's show up,' he once said."

While Natalie was president of the KCHAF, it grew from a struggling nonprofit that could barely raise the funds needed to deliver groceries each week to people with HIV and AIDS. By the time her presidency ended, the group had a pool of steady donors to support the foundation's mission and services. It also added new programs, such as Stockings for a Cause, in which members of the community make creative holiday stockings that are auctioned off to support KCHAF's outreach efforts.

A major financial turnaround for the group came when it received an unexpected donation from an old acquaintance of Natalie. The more she spoke in the community, the more consciousness she raised, and the more donations arrived. One day, she got a call from a woman who had traveled with her on several trips overseas. The woman had heard that Natalie was doing something with an AIDS foundation, and wanted to know more.

Natalie told her about the support groups and the dinners, the groceries and the Christmas gift certificates that the clients received through KCHAF. Two weeks later, Bryson received a $17,000 check in the mail. The woman and her partner donated the money with no strings attached, and they have been benefactors of KCHAF ever since. "I have been so grateful for their generosity and support," says Bryson. "No one does it alone."

The Kitsap Unitarian Universalist Fellowship, where Natalie is a member, also emerged as a source of support and financial backing, as well as a messenger for her causes.

Central to Natalie's support system were the sons that she lost. "I got a PhD in AIDS mothering, I can tell you that. But I got it from the professorship of my six children. They were so support-ive of me, and they were the ones who got me through this."

She keeps a photo of James and a photo of David in her bed-room, and she says hello to them every morning. She lives with their deaths every day. But she doesn't dwell on their passing. She also has pictures in her bedroom of her four living children, Eliza-beth, Muriel, William, and Rebecca. She says good morning to all of them too.

"I'm rarely down. I don't do the 'poor me' thing," she says. She shrugs off the health concerns. She contracted dengue fever while traveling in China, which has left her with residual health issues. And she survived two serious bouts with cancer, one while her sons were ill. Yet Bryson describes herself as the luckiest person in the world. "I've had the highest highs and the lowest lows," she says. "That's called life."

Kitsap County HIV AIDS Foundation
www.kchaf.org

> "There is a connection between faith positions and our impact on the planet."

Creating a Greener, Cleaner Earth

Between a mosque and a Mennonite church in Champaign, Illinois, Muslims and Mennonites are tending a patch of earth together. Some in headscarves and some in modest Mennonite attire, they plant strawberries and tomatoes. Side by side, they weed and water.

Up north in Evanston, the rabbi of the Jewish Reconstructionist Congregation—the nation's greenest worship space, built from recycled steel and wood and committed to the principle of *tikkun olam*, "repairing the world"—brainstorms about how to encourage people to reduce the environmental impact of their bar mitzvah celebrations.

On Chicago's South Side, during a summer of heated gang violence and random shootings, eighteen youth, ranging from fifteen to twenty-one years old tend an urban garden. They're earning money in a summer when jobs are scarce. And they're learning about organics and a rainbow diet in a gritty neighborhood dotted with fast food and liquor stores.

They are all projects of Faith in Place, a Chicago-based nonprofit that partners with religious organizations to promote clean energy and sustainable farming. Clare Butterfield has been leading Faith in Place since 1999 to help people in faith communities reduce their carbon footprint, convert to green energy, and care for the ecology of their neighborhoods.

"Our mission is to help people of faith understand that issues of ecology and economy—of care for Creation—are at the forefront of social justice," says Clare. "We believe in housing the homeless, feeding the hungry, and clothing the naked. But even if we do all those things, and love our brothers and sisters with our whole heart, it will not matter if we neglect the ecological conditions of our beautiful and fragile planet." In eleven years, she and her staff have worked with more than six hundred congregations—Christian, Jewish, Muslim, Hindu, Buddhist, Sikh, Zoroastrian, Bahá'í, and Unitarian Universalist.

"We believe there is a connection between faith positions and our impact on the planet," she says. Clare has worked to build an organization that is kind to the planet and respectful of the humans who inhabit it. Faith in Place reaches out to communities that are both racially and religiously diverse, and employs a diverse staff too. Although the environmental movement has historically been favored by white, middle-class progressives, she works with a full spectrum of people and religious organizations in Greater Chicago.

"It's my genius that I've decided to help a dying planet by hitching my wagon to a dying movement—religion," says Clare. It's a typical Clare comment—unvarnished truth laced with what initially seems like cynicism. But she's more optimist than cynic. That's how she's able to come back to her Chicago offices each day and field the range of phone calls that stream in to Faith in Place. Congregations call for energy audits, information on starting a green team, or advice about renovating their facility to be more energy efficient. Calls come in from congregations that have heard about the organization's Environment 101 workshops. Some inquire about creating urban farmers' markets to bring organics into the inner city. And others have sought help creating winter farmers' markets, featuring meat, cheese, and woolens. Faith in Place advises on funding sources and best practices, so no congregation has to reinvent the green wheel.

In recent years, Faith in Place has also helped congregations come together to do policy advocacy. It's been the next step in the group's evolution. "Ten years ago, we asked people: Is there a connection between our faith and environmental practices? Then we helped people implement those practices," Clare says. Once people internalized those new habits, she pushed people to take the next step. "Well, it's great to use energy-efficient light bulbs," she says, "but why not mandate a higher floor for efficiency?"

Combining practice and policy, Faith in Place is expanding its impact, from the individual congregant and congregations to lawmakers and regulators. In her ten years of environmental work, Clare estimates that her organization has influenced more than a quarter of a million people. She arrives at that figure by calculating that Faith in Place has worked with more than six hundred congregations, averaging four hundred members. "I can still remember when our outreach was in the high one figure," she laughs.

As she begins her second decade at Faith in Place and nears her fiftieth birthday, Clare feels a renewed sense of excitement and inspiration in her work. In her first ten years heading the organization she experienced ups and downs and worries about whether she was making a difference or could continue her work. "It's fun again," she says. The staff has grown to six people, and Clare feels reinvigorated by their successful outreach to new communities.

"I take my inspiration in a lot of ways from the Velvet Revolution and the Solidarity Movement," she says, referring to the nonviolent revolutions in Czechoslovakia and Poland. Even as people waited for the Iron Curtain to fall, says Clare, "they decided to live as if the reality of what they wanted was already here. It showed the power to imagine a different reality and create a different reality."

Taking a page from that book, Clare says that at Faith in Place, they've decided to "obstinately and naively imagine a reality in which people are kind to one another. And we're sincerely curious about a different way of seeing things. So in a tiny way we've created that reality. How could I leave now? It's way too much fun."

Clare grew up in Champaign County on a tree farm. Her father was a professor and an engineer, and he planted trees in orderly rows arranged by species. "I grew up among the trees," she says. "My orientation to place is to Illinois. I know the watershed and the trees. It's where my heart is." As a child, she delighted in walking among the neighbors' farms and surrounding woods. She felt the rhythm of the seasons move across the land and developed a deep feeling for the land's importance and her connection to it.

She attended college at the University of Illinois. And like so many liberal arts majors in the 1970s, she moved on to law school after that. She was drawn to tax law and practiced in that specialty for twelve years, including a four-year stint with the IRS in Washington DC, before she felt the irresistible pull to move back to her home state. The next irresistible pull was to leave the profession entirely.

Clare still thinks that being a tax lawyer is a perfectly good profession. But she started to feel that she wasn't meant to be one. She felt the "vocational tug" to go to divinity school, so she enrolled in Chicago's Meadville Lombard Theological School and became a Unitarian Universalist minister.

During her studies, Clare began a field placement at the Center for Neighborhood Technology (CNT). Founded in 1978, the CNT focuses on sustainable urban living. Clare's job was to reach out to the faith community. She was excited by the mix of community organizing and environmentalism. But, always a questioner, she had some persistent qualms. She wondered why the work didn't take into account people's needs for personal transformation. How, she asked herself, could she pay attention to individuals as religious people and not just as numbers involved in a movement? These "cranky questions," she says, gave rise to the project that became Faith in Place.

Clare and her field supervisor at CNT began to assemble an interfaith group to talk about religious belief and environmental action. "There's a lot of consistency across the faiths on the question of the quality of our relationships and what they are supposed to look like—whether that's Muslim, Buddhist, Jewish, or Baháʼí. All are motivated by respect and care and obligation. And those to me are the foundation of an ecological worldview," she says.

An intellectual with short grey hair and wire-rim glasses, Clare loves to ponder the big questions. But at the same time, she's tried to keep the focus of Faith in Place pragmatic, creating a clearinghouse to make it easier for individuals and congregations to act.

"The environmental hair shirt is something that I try to avoid," she says. "That's a liberal tendency—to find fault with everything." But she would rather see people take small actions than feel paralyzed by the magnitude of the environmental problems the world is facing. For example, rather than giving up coffee entirely, she thinks it's appropriate instead for congregations and individuals to find the most sustainable way to grow and buy coffee.

Then, she hopes, congregations can make larger changes. A congregation that first changes its light bulbs can then ask bigger questions, such as, What is the embedded energy of the products we are using? Embedded energy is the total amount of energy used in a product's life cycle—from mining the raw materials, to manufacturing, assembly, transportation, and finally, its decomposition.

Clare tries to keep her own carbon footprint as small as possible. She lives with her artist husband, Edward Maldonado, in a modest Chicago townhouse. She drives as infrequently as she can, but couldn't travel to far-flung Illinois congregations without a car. So she drives a hybrid Toyota Prius.

She's not a vegetarian. But the meat she eats—about once a week—is locally and humanely raised. She shops at farmers' markets, and her bathtub is crisscrossed with clotheslines, because she tries to limit her use of her energy-hogging clothes dryer to once a week.

"I'm not interested in unproductive guilt," she says. "I want people to understand that the way we've structured our society is unsustainable. So we have to claim our personal integrity." She hopes people will take sustainable options where they exist and when they can afford it. Then they can look for integrity as a faith community. And then the community can see how much societal change it can bring about. Even when those actions don't succeed at first, Clare says, "you still have your personal integrity to fall back on."

Faith in Place was embraced early on by Unitarian Universalist congregations in Illinois. It was a natural connection in many ways. Clare holds a position as a community minister at Unity Temple in Oak Park. And environmental issues have been a priority for UU churches for many years, reflecting the seventh Principle of Unitarian Universalism: "Respect for the interdependent web of all existence of which we are a part."

However, she would never have been content to work just within Unitarian Universalism. And she has built a broad and diverse coalition. The organization's nine-member board represents the Reformed Jewish, Zen Buddhist, United Church of Christ, Episcopalian, Lutheran, Presbyterian, Hindu, Zoroastrian, and Roman Catholic communities.

The board members represent their faith traditions and have helped implement ideas from Faith in Place in their own communities. Clare has learned over the years that it's best to find influence makers within congregations to spread the word about environmentalism rather than finding environmentalists within the congregations. In the past, she had sought out hard-core environmentalists. However, she found that those people could alienate others in their congregations. "There's a type in the environmental movement," she says. A picture of the type quickly comes to mind. Khaki pants. Vegan sandals. A canvas bag. And a particular earnestness.

"Our practices can be off-putting. It's so overwhelming because there are so many things to do," she says. "If you turn someone's trip to the grocery store into a series of unsolvable dilemmas, people will find another issue."

So she has looked for influence makers who can shape opinion and help make the connection between their faith and environmentalism. And then those people can pass out postcards to two or three hundred people to begin a policy campaign. "We have to mainstream it," says Clare. "Some environmentalists hate that, but I don't mind meeting people where they are."

It's an approach Clare learned through hard knocks. She initially began recruiting people from different congregations to create discussion groups called "sustainability circles." She learned that the folks who responded to the call were refugees from their faith groups who were angry at their congregations. They were not the ones to sway others in their communities.

She dismantled the circles and began to work one-on-one within congregations. When the documentary *An Inconvenient Truth* came out in 2006, chronicling Vice President Al Gore's environmental crusade, Clare was able to make the film available to congregations though the affiliation of Faith in Place with the national Interfaith Power and Light movement. Through those screenings, more doors began to open. Congregants became more receptive when she asked whether they had considered adding environmentalism to their social justice portfolios. For many years, she reached out to clergy and laypeople, but as the organization's profile rose, people began to seek her out.

She has hired designated staff to reach into specific communities. For several years, Faith in Place employed a Muslim staff member to build bridges to mosques. One mosque in Bridgeview used the group's resources to help them build a solar hot water system. Another in Willowbrook invited Clare to speak during Ramadan about how religious people can become involved in environmental practices. And for six years, Faith in Place ran a meat co-op that sold *halal* organic meat.

In 2008, Faith in Place hired an African-American staffer to reach out to black churches in the Chicago area. For years, Clare had been trying to do the outreach herself. She was greeted politely but made little headway. But Veronica Kyle did. She had worked for faith-based groups doing social justice and development work in the Caribbean and South Africa for twelve years. She was welcomed by African-American churches with open arms. In just eighteen months, she brought thirty African-American congregations into the Faith in Place fold, primarily from Chicago's South Side. The churches formed Green Teams—and almost immediately began creating jobs for young people.

The first of the jobs projects was a weatherization clinic. Faith in Place trained eighty young people involved in church youth programs to install weather stripping and plastic sheeting in the homes of community members. The kids primarily installed the kits in the homes of elderly residents to retain heat during the cold Chicago winters. The teens received $5 for each kit installed, along with bonuses for high performance. In all, they weather-stripped more than five hundred homes, earning money, developing job skills, and learning about energy conservation in the process.

In the summer of 2010, Faith in Place initiated an inner-city summer jobs program to create an urban community garden. Faith in Place applied for a state grant to create the jobs, combining much-needed summer employment during the hot, violent summer with training on food and gardening.

Six teenagers gather in the 90-degree July heat at Messiah and St. Bartholomew's Episcopal Church on Chicago's South Side. Phillip Mantle, its executive director, gives them a healthy lunch before loading them into a van and driving them to a lush green garden. Sirens and horns drone in the background, but the bustle of the street is out of sight. The garden is tucked behind a rehab center and an ice skating rink in the city's Avalon Park neighborhood.

After they pile out of the van, the three boys and two girls slip on blue Faith in Place T-shirts. Brittany and Angel walk across the lot together to weed tomato plants in raised beds. Kyle weeds cabbage plants and flowers, while Rodney moves from bed to bed, watering vegetables with a hose.

It's the first summer job for Demetriux, seventeen. He said that Mantle had told him about the opportunity one afternoon as he walked past St. Bartholomew's, heading home from playing basketball in the park. He had never gardened before. The closest he had come was cutting the grass. Twenty-one-year-old Kyle does landscaping work, so the gardening experience dovetails nicely with his other job. "I like this kind of work," he says. "It's quiet, and I can think." The girls, both fifteen, had planted container gardens last summer at the Avalon Park Community Church, where they met Veronica Kyle, who works with Faith in Place.

Samantha House is overseeing the gardening work. During the school year, she's a mental health counselor in the Chicago schools. She advises the young people on their daily assignments, with the help of a master gardener who oversees the whole site. And she provides daily lessons for the youth on healthy eating and the environment.

"How many calories do you need for a day?" she asked. The guesses came in tentative bursts. "Nine?" "Sixty?" All guesses were a far cry from the two to three thousand calories the average teen needs each day. She is helping the youth understand how to make good choices, what *organic* means, and how to eat across the food rainbow. She showed the youth the movie *Food, Inc.* to get them thinking about where their food comes from, whether it is a piece of fruit, a hamburger, or a bag of chips. "These are teens who don't know a lot about the earth and why it's important," says House. "In the city, you forget about nature."

The program also trains the youth to show up for their jobs on time and to learn how it feels to put in a day of hard work. Each Friday, they work with the younger kids in day camp at St. Bartholomew's. Each of the youth keeps a journal about the gardening, the work, and their food and nutrition classes. And they're all looking forward to the September harvest, when they'll share the food they've grown with the church and the community.

The Avalon Park garden is one of four summer job/urban garden projects that Faith in Place ran in the summer of 2010. To qualify for employment, each of the youth has to be from a family living below the poverty line, and each will earn about $3,000 for the summer.

Faith in Place also runs after-school programs to increase the environmental literacy of urban youth. Targeted primarily at Latino youth, the drop-in program teaches kids about a wide range of skills, from gardening to composting to raising honeybees.

Clare is fiercely committed to environmentalism and interfaith collaboration at a time when neither practice appears to be going well on a world scale. As the Mennonites and Muslims garden together in Champaign, a project of the Central Illinois office of Faith in Place, New Yorkers are fiercely opposing the construction of a Muslim Community Center a few blocks from Ground Zero in Lower Manhattan. Like many cities around the country, Chicago experienced one of its hottest summers on record in 2010, confirming Clare's belief that climate change is bad and getting worse, and that there's no indication that we are making any progress to combat the phenomenon.

Yet she remains energized and even hopeful. "I'm sure people who lived through the plague thought it was the end of the world, but it wasn't," she says. And she believes that Faith in Place has made a difference in its ten years. It has put the environmental issue on the map as something faith communities can tackle. It has encouraged individuals to examine and reduce their environmental impact. And it has begun to influence environmental policy by lobbying the Illinois legislature on issues related to clean energy and solar power, and the federal government on carbon caps.

Each year in late winter, Faith in Place staff coordinate an annual policy workshop as the Illinois General Assembly prepares to get underway. And each spring, they join the Illinois Environmental Council lobby day at the state capitol in Springfield.

She would like to expand the organization's reach beyond their Chicago base. In January 2010, Faith in Place opened a Central Illinois office to expand outreach downstate. She also hired Brian

Sauder as the outreach and policy coordinator for Central Illinois and the policy coordinator for the state. A member of First Mennonite Church of Champaign, he's directing his efforts toward congregations that have long felt out of reach to Chicago headquarters.

"Traditionally, our collective skews progressive," says Clare. "I'd love to see how far toward center-right we can go." Bringing in congregations outside of the traditionally liberal Chicago area is key to that effort. "Brian is much more likely to speak to a group where there are a large number of skeptics about climate change."

Another of Clare's latest efforts is to pilot green technologies. Faith in Place board member Rashi Ramaswamy is an architect who developed a prototype for a Mod Pod—a sub-irrigation system that efficiently brings water into compact urban gardens. Six Faith in Place member congregations are giving the Mod Pod a trial run in their urban gardens. And Clare has one in her own patio garden, where she grows lettuce, beans, cucumbers, and tomatoes.

The Mod Pod aligns with the organization's growing concern with water. The staff is creating a new curriculum for faith communities to increase their water literacy. "In most traditions, water has a life-giving sacred role," Clare says. At the same time, the availability and safety of water in many communities is threatened by climate change. The water curriculum will explore water's spiritual, scientific, and policy issues.

Clare harvests the last of her patio crop as she puts the final touches on planning the fall Harvest Celebration hosted by Faith in Place. The eleventh annual dinner is a fundraiser and a celebration of another year of bringing more congregations to the table to examine their impact on the earth.

The 2010 Harvest Dinner drew 140 guests to the Chicago Cultural Center. Among them were teens who had participated in the summer youth garden program. As one of their final projects, they had created a cookbook. Each of the night's guests received a copy to take home.

Guests browsed the silent auction items: green products, weeks at vacation homes, gift baskets, and a chance to be guest chef for the day at the restaurant of Chicago celebrity chef Charlie Trotter. The program began with prayers. A Lutheran board member of Faith in Place sang grace in a booming baritone. A Zoroastrian board member offered a blessing from his tradition. A rabbi blessed the bread, and an African-American minister and the Hindu board chair gave prayers before the meal—locally raised organic chicken, mushroom strudel, and seasonal local vegetables.

The centerpiece of this year's Harvest Dinner was an architectural competition for green religious buildings. Models of the competing designs were stationed around the hall. Three entries won $5,000 cash prizes donated to the competition in the categories of best multi-use building, best freestanding religious structure, and best multi-congregation design.

"Our goal with the competition has been to develop ideas that will help congregations considering significant remodeling or new construction," says Clare. "Ultimately, we want to see the religious building transformed from a burden to congregations to a vehicle for solving the many problems religious bodies address as part of their missions—from social services to education to civic engagement and more. Enabling these buildings to be used fully every day was key."

From ticket sales and bidding on the silent auction, the Harvest Dinner raised $36,000 to support the work of Faith in Place. Clare was gratified by the fundraising and moved by the diversity of faith the event attracts each year, as Christians, Hindus, Muslims, Zoroastrians, Buddhists, Bahá'ís, and Unitarian Universalists gather. As she surveyed the crowd, she visualized the many barriers that have been broken in her community to bring these people together for a night of celebration.

"Chicago is famously segregated but famously diverse," she says. "I've operated from the theory that people are eager for opportunities to take barriers down and meet one another.

"There is no other. That's a myth. I believe that theologically and socially. That which is divine is in all things."

Faith in Place
www.faithinplace.org

"I believe this is one small and fragile world that belongs to all of us."

Building Bridges Across Race

Nelson Mandela gave Janice Marie Johnson an unusual gift. He gave her a word.

It was 1994, and Mandela was visiting the United States for the first time after serving twenty-seven years in a South African prison for his efforts to dismantle his country's oppressive apartheid system. Janice had been a fan of Mandela for as long as she could remember, and she dreamed of meeting him.

Her father, a diplomat, arranged for her to attend a dinner in Mandela's honor in Washington DC. To Janice's surprise and delight, she was seated at the same table as her hero. She was struck by his interest in the others at the table. He did not spend the evening discussing his own staggering accomplishments— leading the dismantling of apartheid or receiving the Nobel Peace Price the year before. Instead, he wanted to hear others describe themselves. He was an extraordinary listener.

Janice told Mandela about her life. He listened carefully, and then he told her that he knew what she was. She was a bridge builder, and Mandela said that a word from his South African language, Nguni, described her—*masakhane*. It means, "Let us build together."

"The word was such a gift to me that I chose to take it as my maxim," says Janice. "Building bridges is the essence of who I am."

More than fifteen years after meeting Mandela, Janice accepted a position with the Unitarian Universalist Association to work on anti-racism, anti-oppression, and multicultural growth within the denomination. It is the culmination of decades of work in Janice's professional and personal life to build bridges among people of every religion, race, and ethnicity.

Janice finds her work exciting and invigorating, and at times painstaking and slow. Progress is often incremental and difficult to measure. That makes success stories about creating welcoming, diverse congregations all the more worth sharing and celebrating. "It's long-haul work, and it takes patience," she says. And it is work that has evolved for her from the bridges she has built in her own life. Her professional work and her volunteer work eventually merged into one. "I knew I would not be complete until I was doing the work I loved to do," Janice says. "I loved my volunteer work, and when that became my professional work, it was a wonderful thing."

Janice's job involves finding ways to expand the UUA's capacity to invite and include people of diverse races and ethnicities within its liberal religious tradition. "I believe in Unitarian Universalism. It is where my heart lies. Everything I do is around my understanding of social justice in a religious context," she says. "I believe this is one small and fragile world that belongs to all of us."

Janice Marie Johnson has seen the world she wants to build.

In that world, people of every skin color live together in harmony. Children from different cultures sit beside each other in school and play together at recess. They call each other by their given names, no matter how long or foreign-sounding to their own ears. Their teachers, like them, are of many races and religions. That's the world she grew up in.

Janice was born in Jamaica with her twin sister Hope. The girls' parents were among the first people of color in post-Colonial Jamaica to break into the professional class. Janice calls them "first-generation, dark-skinned Jamaican success stories." Their ancestors came to Jamaica from Africa on slave ships. And their grandparents rose as high as they could on the island to become civil servants. But Janice and Hope's parents broke through.

Their mom, Pamela Rogers Johnson, studied medicine in Jamaica and Scotland and became a neurologist, specializing in the treatment of slow viral infections. Their dad, Keith Johnson, studied at Columbia and Oxford universities and became a diplomat, working first at the United Nations as a demographer, then as a Jamaican diplomat, serving as general consul, and then as Jamaican ambassador to many countries, including the United States.

Their parents' careers moved the family around the world. Although she says she is culturally Caribbean, Janice calls herself a child of the world and an internationalist. Janice and Hope were educated in the United Nations International School System. One year, they would be in school in Europe, the next in Asia or South America. They lived in Thailand, India, France, West Germany, England, Japan, Brazil, Argentina, Kenya, Sierra Leon, Cameroon, and Sweden, among other countries. Wherever they went, the twins entered a UN school and knew which page to turn to in their books. The students and the teachers in each school were from many countries and of many races. "I grew up in this crucible of equality," she says. "When I look at my kindergarten pictures, it was as multicultural and multinational as anything."

When she entered college, however, that world of racial innocence came to a crashing end. Janice and Hope flew to New York in the early 1970s to attend Fordham University. That was in the days when people dressed up to fly on airplanes. The two well-dressed young women were picked up at the airport by their father's driver. He drove to an apartment that the Johnson family kept on Manhattan's East Side in the exclusive Sutton Place neighborhood.

The white doorman of the building watched as Hope and Janice stepped out of the chauffeur-driven car. But rather than opening the main door to the apartment building, the doorman escorted the twins to the building's service entrance. They followed the corridor and came to a room full of the building's garbage. Welcome to New York.

Racism became a new part of Janice's life. She had come from a world of privilege and equality, and now she had trouble hailing a taxi. At Fordham, Janice saw people struggle to discern who she was. "We didn't present like people who looked like us," she says. "We were well-traveled, and we lived on Sutton Place. It was difficult to be experienced as people of color."

Janice was not wholly ignorant of racism. Back in Jamaica, she had experienced the island version of discrimination, which she calls "shadism." Shadism favors people with light skin over dark. "I remember people talking about the 'paper bag test,'" she says. "If your skin was no darker than a paper bag, you would be accepted." Janice has a deep-brown skin color, like both her parents. Her father resisted social pressures to marry a light-skinned woman, Janice says. "My father was so proud that he married dark!"

Janice began to build bridges in college. She joined the black student union, and triple-majored in black studies, sociology, and philosophy. And she graduated with a fierce determination to be herself, no matter what expectations people had of her when they saw the color of her skin.

During job interviews, she was counseled by some interviewers, including African-American women, to cut and straighten her hair. Janice has never straightened her hair; she wears it in long dreadlocks. And she shuns suits, which she associates with colonialism. She favors black skirts and shirts, topped by colorful jackets and chunky jewelry, such as an orange and silver necklace she found in Afghanistan. "I love color with a backdrop of black," she says.

Looking back, Janice can see how every step of her life and career lead toward her multicultural work at the UUA. For most of the 1980s, she worked as a textbook editor in New York, concentrating on books focused on multiculturalism, foreign languages, and environmental studies.

She married her childhood sweetheart from Jamaica, a graphic artist named Mark Huie. They lived together in New York, where Hope also lived with her husband. Janice and Mark had a baby daughter, Lehna, in 1988. When Lehna was six weeks old, Mark had a sudden heart attack and died. "I really felt as if my soul mate was gone," says Janice.

She held his funeral at the Community Church of New York, Unitarian Universalist. It was the same church where Mark and Janice had gone for their premarital counseling, before being married at a UU church in Maryland. "I needed a farewell ceremony for him that was as poignant and memorable as our marriage ceremony, so I told folks the funeral had to be at Community Church," says Janice. She joined the church two years later and began her journey toward working with the UUA on diversity issues.

Life after Mark began to change quickly for Janice. Unable to afford their apartment alone, she and Lehna moved in with Hope and her husband and their new baby, Jova, just six months younger than Lehna.

Janice surprised her publishing co-workers by leaving her stable job to open a travel agency with Hope. Janice told them she had to do what she loved. Her husband's sudden death showed her dramatically that she had to live the life she dreamed about in the present moment. "Tomorrow is not promised to us," she told them. "I have a dream, and I have to follow it now."

Drawing on their international upbringing, Janice and Hope established a travel agency that specialized in multinational itineraries and environmentally responsible travel. As they opened their fledgling office in Hope's apartment, they stumbled upon their first client in a bridge-building moment so typical of Janice's life.

The two sisters were riding in an elevator in a Manhattan office building where they had gone to get their license to operate a travel agency. Also in the elevator were three men speaking German, who wondered how they were going to make it across town to get to their next meeting on time. Having lived and studied in Germany, Hope and Janice understood every word. Janice told them they would never make it on time if they took a taxi, but that she would be happy to escort them to the subway station, to midtown, and to the building where their meeting was being held.

The men had little time to think. Should they trust these two black women speaking German? They agreed to let Janice escort them and arrived at their meeting in the nick of time. As it turns out, the men were executives in a German securities business who traveled extensively. They immediately chose the Johnsons' business as their travel agency.

The sisters built their business, eventually selling it to a larger agency. Hope divorced. And the two sisters rented a house with the option to buy it together in Brooklyn's Park Slope neighborhood. "We formed a blended family so we could raise our daughters together in one house," says Janice. Together, they took their daughters to Community Church, where Unitarian Universalism assumed growing significance in both their lives.

Hope decided to go to divinity school and become a Unitarian Universalist minister, serving both in parish ministry and as an active ministerial leader within the UUA. Janice became an active lay leader at Community Church. In addition, she left the travel business to find work that felt more socially responsible.

Janice began to teach courses in cross-cultural communication and conflict management at New York's New School University, and she joined the Morningside Center for Teaching Social Responsibility, through which she worked with the New York City public schools to teach peer mediation and conflict resolution and to advance "peaceable schools." "I was working on creating community that helps students learn better," she says. "Students learn better when they feel safe, respected, and loved. It was very meaningful work." And the work spurred her to earn a masters degree in conflict resolution from Skidmore College.

At the same time, Janice's volunteer efforts increased. She became active in the UU District of Metro New York. And at Community Church, she co-founded the UUA's first committee on diversity, which grew to include anti-racism work.

Both Hope and Janice began to command the attention of the UUA's national leadership. In 2006, the UUA's then-president, Bill Sinkford, presented Janice and Hope with the Association's President's Award for Volunteer Service. Typically, the award is given to an individual. But Sinkford said that he was "pushing the limit . . . and presenting a 'two-fer.'" A list of all their accomplishments, he said, would take too much time, but he presented a sample of their support of Unitarian Universalism: "Janice Marie Johnson has served on the Ministerial Fellowship Committee Board of Review, as a trustee of the Mountain Retreat and Learning Center, as a trustee in our UU United Nations Office, on the Commission on Appraisal, and as president of DRUUMM [Diverse and Revolutionary Unitarian Universalist Multicultural Ministries]. The Reverend Hope Johnson has served on the UUA Nominating Committee, the Anti-Racism Anti-Oppression Multicultural Committee of the UU Ministers Association, on the Family Matters Task Force, as a Jubilee World trainer, and as an adult at-large member of the YRUU Council." And beyond all that, Sinkford said, what he valued most is "the faithfulness with which they both hold the vision of the beloved community that inspires this community wherever they are present."

Around the same time that they received the volunteer award, the leadership of Community Church asked Janice if she would join their staff as the Director of Religious Education. That position grew from a part-time job educating the children to a full-time position as Director of Lifespan Religious Education, serving members of all ages, with an emphasis on social responsibility.

She also traveled to conduct anti-racism seminars for youth and adults. She gained valuable experience at holding difficult conversations. And at one meeting, she also gained another daughter. Janice was leading a seminar at a Unitarian Universalist center. She struggled through a week of uncomfortable and unwelcoming experiences. Amid the awkwardness, one young white woman reached out to Janice when others wouldn't. She wanted to talk about racism and power. Janice was touched by her insight and her kindness. "I told her whenever you come to New York, I will take care of you," Janice said. "Now I call her my Brooklyn daughter."

Caitlin calls Janice her "Brooklyn mama." Janice welcomed her into her family, along with Hope, Lehna, and Jova. When Caitlin came to New York City to attend college, Janice hired her part-time in the Community Church Sunday school. And there was always room in the Park Slope house for her when college life was too tough, and she needed a home and a hug. A decade after they met, Caitlin still considers Janice one of her two moms.

In the meantime, Janice was becoming a part of the ministry team at Community Church and was happily enmeshed in the community she loved. So when a call came for her to join the UUA as director of the Office of Racial and Ethnic Concerns, she had some soul searching to do. "It is hard to leave a place of employment when you know people really care about you. And when it's your church. I cried. I prayed. It was a heart-wrenching decision-making process. And yet, I saw this opportunity to serve the larger faith," recalls Janice.

She knew she could remain an active member of Community Church. And at the same time she could throw herself into the critical work of helping the larger denomination become more welcoming to people of all races and ethnicities. The UUA has a controversial history with anti-racism and anti-oppression work, dating back to the late 1960s, when a so-called Black Empowerment Controversy divided the Association about how to approach racial justice. Janice knew that her job would not be easy.

A year into that job, the position grew to become director of the Office of Multicultural Growth and Witness. In addition to addressing concerns about race and ethnicity, the job now also encompasses welcoming lesbian, gay, bisexual, and transgender people. "I provide leadership, guide strategic initiatives, and develop programs and services that expand Unitarian Universalist congregations' capacity to welcome, include, and meet the ministerial needs of people of diverse races and ethnicities seeking a liberal religious community of love and justice," says Janice. "I support our congregational professional and lay religious leaders in developing cross-cultural knowledge and skills that foster multicultural growth and ministries in Unitarian Universalism at the congregational, district, regional, and national levels. It is huge. It really is huge."

Before Nelson Mandela gave Janice a word, the pope gave her a gift.

While her father was serving as Jamaica's ambassador to the Vatican in the late 1970s, Pope John Paul II invited him and his family to visit for an afternoon. Janice was nervous at the prospect. She walked through Vatican City with her family, eyeing the striped stockings and colorful uniforms of the Swiss Guard, turned to her father, and said, "Daddy, what do you say to a pope?"

Without hesitating, her father replied, "What do you say to anyone? That's what you say to the pope."

It's a lesson Janice has never forgotten. She watched her father treat the pope with great respect, and it was the same respect he afforded everyone—staff at hotels, the man who drove his car. That day, she says, she made the connection that "wherever you fit into society, you are of worth."

She remembers Pope John Paul II as an extraordinary man. She was impressed by his sense of humor, his warmth, and his multilingual skills. And she was struck that, like Nelson Mandela decades later, he was interested in learning about her. He had done his homework before they arrived. He asked her mother questions about her medical work and her hobbies, tennis and badminton. He asked Hope and Janice about their school and their teachers. "He made us at ease," says Janice. "He was a warm-hearted human being."

"I learned that it was not necessary to agree with someone's politics to be at ease with them," says Janice. Echoing the famous words of Francis David, the sixteenth-century founder of the Unitarian Church of Transylvania, she adds, "It helped me appreciate that we need not think alike to love alike."

It's an idea that still informs all her work: "We are all so multifaceted. We can disagree and still love each other."

Janice is involved in many projects at the UUA. She trains congregations and districts in anti-racism and anti-oppression, helping groups to examine and analyze historical and institutional racism in the United States. "No two days are alike!" she says.

With Hope, Janice has helped organize an annual civil rights tour of the Deep South. The two sisters became involved in that project after deciding they didn't know enough about the southern United States, so they took a tour organized by the Meadville Lombard Theological School, a Unitarian Universalist seminary in Chicago. The school was not certain whether it could continue to run the tours, so Hope and Janice asked what they could do to help keep them alive. The sisters became part of a planning team to resurrect the program. The first one they ran attracted Rev. Bill Sinkford, then president of the UUA; Gini Courter, the UUA moderator; and Rev. Mark Morrison-Reed, a retired Unitarian Universalist minister and scholar, known for researching the history of black Unitarians and Universalists. "I couldn't believe he came on the tour," says Janice about Morrison-Reed. "I had the belief that he could teach it!"

The trip unites the travel agent in Janice with the social justice activist. It's a pilgrimage that takes in iconic sites in the civil rights movement. "You go to Birmingham, and you have a sense of the dogs just about to tear your skin. You walk over the Edmund Pettus Bridge [in Selma, Alabama], and you get an understanding of the South that I could not have imagined. You go to the Voting Rights Museum, and you realize that it wasn't that long ago that black people didn't have a vote." The tour also focuses on Unitarian Universalists such as Rev. James Reeb, who died fighting for civil rights. "I can't imagine going to many cities in this country where people know the name James Reeb and have a sense of his story," says Janice. "But in Selma, he is a hero. Everyone in Selma celebrates his legacy and his memory. It's extraordinary."

Much of her work centers around providing leadership to develop programs that support the ministerial needs of people of different races and ethnicities and that support ministers of different backgrounds. For example, each year she hosts a gathering of UU ministers and religious professionals of color for a three-day retreat to help them build community.

Another community is a group of twenty-four congregations that Janice calls "our multicultural learning communities." Under the leadership of Rev. Alicia Forde, they gather in monthly telephone conferences to share best practices and struggles and to learn from one another.

The Office of Multicultural Growth and Witness also created an initiative called the Multicultural Growth Consultation. It used an appreciative inquiry approach—which focuses on what an organizations does well—as it followed ten congregations on "multicultural ministry journeys." The consultation helped them conduct focused conversations to determine how the ministers were doing and identify best practices for multicultural ministry. The consultation created a road map, Janice says, to help congregations become justice-centered, inclusive, multicultural faith communities.

"I believe that Unitarian Universalism is big enough for many," she says. "I really want to see it grow. I want to see more Unitarian Universalists in our world. We want beloved community, and we want to build it. The fact that we don't quite know how to do it doesn't mean that we shouldn't do it. I know we can. I go back to that picture of me and my classmates in kindergarten. I have experienced that kind of community like it's the most natural thing in the world, and I aspire to recreate it."

Janice's latest and perhaps most ambitious and passionate project is creating a Multicultural Learning and Leadership Institute within the UUA. It will be a place for ministers and congregants to enhance skills for engaging with people of many backgrounds. She is developing the curriculum and creating training in the form of online webinars as well as in-person intensive courses.

"I work with a team—an incredible staff team, who are a blessing. Each one brings tremendous gifts," says Janice, and each of them is helping to develop the core curriculum. She sees the institute as a way to expand the conversation about being welcoming to every culture deeper and wider—first throughout the UUA and then beyond.

The institute is also a way for Janice to continue to build bridges—bigger and wider and open to more people. And she hopes it will be a way for people to come together to share their stories about their own backgrounds and of what works in their communities.

"It is important to tell our stories," says Janice. "Storytelling is as old as time. It is how community is captured and how community is sustained across the generations. When you know someone's story, how do you not love them? How do you not forgive each other and begin again in love? How do we not recognize the divine spark in each and every one? When we know each other's stories, we don't have to do so much of this anti-oppression work."

Janice is a woman of so many stories. She will always hold dear the story of Nelson Mandela and the treasured gift he gave her. "The notion of building together with a collaborative spirit is very real to me," she says. "It is the essence of who I am." *Masakhane.*

Unitarian Universalist Association Office of Multicultural Growth and Witness
www.uua.org/multiculturalism

"After an unspeakable atrocity had taken place between two cultures, children decided to exchange crayons and drawings and restart what their parents had destroyed."

Rebuilding a War-Torn World

On the morning of August 6, 1945, four hundred students of the Honkawa Elementary School in Hiroshima, Japan, sat at desks to begin their school day. As the children settled down for their morning lessons, the American B-29 bomber, the *Enola Gay*, flew overhead and dropped an atomic bomb. The blast produced the bomb's iconic mushroom cloud over the city, and incinerated the schoolchildren and eighty thousand of their fellow citizens instantly.

Fourteen months later in Washington DC, two American admirals in full regalia posed with a smiling, elegantly dressed woman about to cut into an elaborate angel-food cake. Swirls of angel-food puffs towered over the cake to create a giant mushroom cloud pastry, the centerpiece of a celebration of the atomic-bomb task force.

Rev. A. Powell Davies, the minister of All Souls Church, Unitarian, in Washington DC, saw the newspaper photo and was outraged by its insensitivity. The next Sunday, he preached about the bombings and the photos; the sermon garnered publicity around the world.

Rev. Davies's address, "Lest the Living Forget," spurred the children of his church to action, setting off a chain of events that, more than sixty years later, continues to foster a spirit of connection and kindness. It changed the lives of children on both sides of the world.

"I have with me here in the pulpit this morning a page from a newspaper. From a very fine newspaper. It contains a picture—as it seems to me, an utterly loathsome picture. If I spoke as I feel I would call it obscene," Davies preached on the November morning in 1946. "How would it seem in Hiroshima, or Nagasaki, to know that Americans make cakes—of angel-food puffs—in the image of that terrible, diabolical thing that brought sudden death to thousands of their friends, and a lingering, loathsome death to thousands of others? It is a crime—a crime against whatever may be left of decency here in America—to do this incredible thing."

Davies continued, "If I had the authority of a priest of the Middle Ages, I would call down the wrath of God upon such an obscenity. I would damn to hell these people of callous conscience, these traitors to humanity who would participate in such a monstrous betrayal of everything for which the brokenhearted of the world are waiting. But—perhaps fortunately—I have no such authority. And so I only pray that God will give me patience and compassion. That I may be just—and merciful—and humble. And still speak the truth that is in me."

Davies's invective was picked up by newspapers and magazines in the United States and around the world. *Time* magazine called the sermon "probably the harshest words ever spoken of a dessert." The article was read by Howard Bell, an official in General Douglas MacArthur's provisional government in Japan. As forceful as Davies's sermon had been, Bell believed it was not strident enough. Bell wrote Davies a letter telling him he understood that Davies had to soften his words and "to make some concessions to the proprieties of public utterance."

Bell also told Davies that the children of Hiroshima were suffering. Most of the Honkawa Elementary School's twelve hundred students had been evacuated from the city before the bombing. But after the devastation, they slowly began to return, dutifully reporting each day to the burned-out skeleton of the reinforced-concrete building to try "to learn democracy." The school had no heat, Bell wrote, and the children's cheeks were blue and their hands were purple. They had no school supplies. Bell had scrounged up a table and benches. But the students had nothing else. Bell asked Davies if he could help.

Davies presented the plight of the Japanese children to the All Souls congregation in a February 1947 sermon called "In Reply to a Letter from Japan." The children of the congregation set out to help the children of Hiroshima. They collected more than half a ton of supplies, including pencils, crayons, paper, erasers, and paper clips.

The task then fell to Davies's assistant, Jane Pfeiffer, to find a way to get the supplies to Japan. She packaged them in wooden crates marked for two schools, the Honkawa Elementary School and the Fukuro-Machi Elementary School, and the Ninoshima Orphanage. Pfeiffer shipped them to MacArthur's headquarters under a special War Department permit. It was the first civilian package to be received there after World War II, Pfeiffer recalls. The packages arrived just before Christmas 1947. They were accompanied by a letter from military headquarters that read, "This present was sent from your friends in All Souls' Church of Washington DC, with deep sincereness. Sympathizing that you, who may have lost your homes and parents due to the atomic bomb, would be feeling very lonely without a Christmas present, they have asked me to deliver these boxes to you before Christmas. Please accept them as tokens of deep friendship."

Several months later, a return package arrived in Washington, addressed to the children of All Souls. Inside were several Japanese comic books, two rag dolls, seventy-five thank-you letters letters from the children of Fukuro-Machi School of Hiroshima, and a thank-you letter from the Ninoshima Orphanage. One sixth-grade girl wrote, "When we were given the articles, I felt my heart beating. . . . There was no glass in the windows of our school last year . . . and we were studying trembling in the cold wind, but the school has completely changed. It will become cold from now on in Japan, but I will worry about that no more."

The package also contained a book of forty-eight watercolor paintings and crayon drawings by the children of Honkawa Elementary. The pictures were astonishing. Despite the atrocities these children had witnessed, their pictures showed scenes of beauty and joy—a boat at sea, a baseball cap, kites flying, peace doves, the green mountains of Hiroshima, cherry blossoms, girls in kimonos. Each bore the artist's name and age—some as young as seven, a few as old as twelve. And each had a title, such as "World of Sky and Water," "Peace—Japan," and "Friends of America."

After the bombing of Hiroshima and Nagasaki, a new form of artwork emerged. Called *hibakusha* art, it is the art of the survivors, and for many Japanese it is sacred. Most hibakusha art is by adults and depicts gruesome apocalyptic images of bombed-out Japan. The children's creations could not be more different. Robert M. Hardies, the senior minister at All Souls since 2001, describes them as "vibrant, colorful depictions of life abundant."

"How can the drawings betray so much hope?" Hardies wonders. He believes they are nothing short of a miracle in the midst of ruin. A miracle made possible by "a gesture of solidarity from children half a world away."

After the paintings and drawings arrived in Washington, they enjoyed a brief popularity. The children of All Souls answered each of the seventy-five letters from the Japanese children. The art and gifts were exhibited at the church, and the U.S. government sent them on a year-long tour.

The All Souls children started a second collection for their new Japanese friends. This time, they collected baseball bats, mitts, and balls, along with table tennis paddles and tennis equipment. The gifts were precious to the children and the city. One of the first buildings constructed among Hiroshima's ruins was the Children's Cultural Hall of Hiroshima. The city put the donated equipment on display there in a 1949 ceremony. And Hiroshima mayor Shinzo Hamai sent All Souls a letter expressing his "heartfelt gratitude."

When the artwork was returned to All Souls after the tour, the church staff put it away for safekeeping. For many years, the paintings and drawings languished in the congregation's safe, collecting dust next to the communion silver. Tucked away and safe from harm, they were forgotten. For decades, many new members of All Souls did not know they existed, although on occasion, a Japanese tourist would knock on the doors of the church, asking, "Is this the church with the Hiroshima children's drawings?" In 2005, however, a group set out to bring the miraculous pieces back to public life.

Rev. Davies was a charismatic and influential minister. He was committed to advancing Unitarianism and social activism. Though he died in 1957, All Souls maintains an A. Powell Davies Memorial Committee that furthers his work and carries out his legacy. In 2005, that group turned its attention to the Hiroshima children's art. Then-church administrator Mel Hardy formed a group to restore and frame it. Paul Pfeiffer, husband of Davies's assistant Jane Pfeiffer, served on both the Davies Memorial Committee and the restoration group.

Pfeiffer is also a World War II veteran. At the time of the Hiroshima bombings, he served as a lieutenant commander in the communications office of the U.S.S. *Vincennes*, which fought in Okinawa and Iwo Jima and bombed Tokyo.

More than sixty years after the children's artwork arrived in Washington, Pfeiffer is still moved by it. "All these fool adults were killing each other with atom bombs, and these little children were making all these drawings," he said. "There's no sign of violence in these paintings. It's loving stuff. Kid's stuff. What fools we adults are. The beauty of these paintings is it was kid to kid."

The restoration committee raised about $15,000, partly from the A. Powell Davies Committee and partly from the Beckner-All

Souls Advancement Fund. The money was used to restore and frame the original art and to create high-quality enhanced reproductions. In 2009, they were put on display in the church's Pierce Hall for public viewing.

The restorations have gone a long way toward keeping the story of the children's art and their trans-Pacific friendship alive.

In the spring of 2009, All Souls unveiled the restored art and held a Cherry Blossom special service during the city's National Cherry Blossom Festival. It was a fitting time for the tribute—cherry blossoms are depicted in the children's paintings and Washington's cherry blossoms have a special connection to All Souls. The city's first two cherry blossom trees were planted in 1912 by First Lady Helen Taft, wife of President William Howard Taft, and a member of All Souls. The trees were a gift from the Japanese ambassador to the United States.

Ichiro Fujisake, the current Japanese ambassador, attended the 2009 service and ceremony and viewed the revered artwork. A youth choir from the All Souls Unitarian Church in Tulsa sang, and the Shizumi Kodomo Dance Troupe performed. Fujisake listened to Rev. Hardies's sermon recounting the story set in motion by the mushroom-cloud cake. Hardies said that he sees a profound theological message in the story of the children's art. "After an unspeakable atrocity had taken place between two cultures, children decided to exchange crayons and drawings and restart what their parents had destroyed," Hardies says. "It was an effort by children to redeem the legacy of devastation that we have left them."

"Friends," Hardies preached, "the mushroom cloud remains an iconic image of our age, threatening us with our own annihilation. But there is another image that is also unique to this age, an image that didn't exist before man's exploration of space. And it is the image of planet Earth taken from space, the image of Earth, a blue-green orb, harmonious, flourishing, fragile. These two images—the mushroom cloud and Earth cradled in space—sum up the choice of our generation. We must choose between the bomb and the blue-green Earth."

Hardies notes that the name of the Washington church derives from a quote by the nineteenth-century Unitarian theologian William Ellery Channing, who said, "I am a living member of the great family of all souls." The story of the Hiroshima art, Hardies says, is a way to bear witness to what Channing said.

The Hiroshima paintings and drawings no longer hide in a closet. Their restoration has brought the story back to life and they embarked on a worldwide tour, heading back to their birthplace in Hiroshima.

Documentary filmmaker Bryan Reichardt went with them. In *Pictures of a Hiroshima Schoolyard*, he interviews seventeen of the hibakusha who made the art, now in their seventies. The film's producer, Shizumi Shigeto Manale, first saw the drawings and paintings in 2007 with three hibakusha who had traveled to Washington. "I knew immediately that these drawings had to be preserved in order to keep alive not only the hopes and dreams of the artists, but the history of a tragic historical period recorded by these children," she said. "To me, these drawings and calligraphy by Hiroshima schoolchildren are evidence of a miracle that opens the door to another level of human kindness."

The drawings and paintings returned Hiroshima in July 2010. The filmmakers and a delegation from All Souls, including Rev. Hardies and six church members, accompanied them to the Honkawa schoolyard.

The framed pieces were hung in a memorial in the Honkawa school. Seventeen of the children who had created the pieces returned to their former school to see their original art for the first time in more than sixty years. The artists eyed their own works with reverence. They welcomed their American guests, and through translators, recounted their memories of why they had drawn and painted them.

One woman recounted drawing cherry blossom trees. The American delegation listened with wonder as she explained that in the spring after the bomb had dropped, some cherry blossom trees survived to bloom again. Her childhood sketch was not a memory of life before the bomb but of nature rejuvenating itself after its destruction.

A man explained that he had painted a baseball cap with the letter K on it because someone had brought the cap back from Hawaii, and he treasured it.

Judith Bauer was among the All Souls delegation. In her early seventies, she is a contemporary of the Honkawa artists. She has a clear memory of the bomb being dropped when she was a child in New Haven. The attack carried none of the glory and celebrations of the end of the war in Europe. No confetti. No dancing in the streets. She remembers quiet.

She also remembers that in her African-American community, many felt that the bomb would not have been dropped on white Europeans. It was dropped on people who looked different and lived differently from "Americans," and that has always affected her perception of Hiroshima.

Alongside the Japanese artists, the Americans from All Souls held a press conference for the Japanese media the day after the opening of the exhibit. They presented the Honkawa school with a set of reproductions of the art and answered questions from the press. Again and again, reporters asked the All Souls members why they had kept the pieces all this time and why they had spent so much money having them restored.

The Americans worked hard to answer the questions. "We talked about social justice and how important it is," says Bauer. "We stressed the importance of children, of our own children and of other people's children. And we told them how much hope was involved in this project—that hope survives, and decency survives."

The All Souls group also visited the Ninoshima Orphanage, which had received crates of drawing supplies and had sent a thank-you letter. It sits on an island in the Seto Inland Sea, a half-hour ferry ride from Hiroshima. Bauer's most powerful memory of the trip was visiting the memorial there and browsing through a book, written in English, that catalogued the names and stories of the children who had "met the bomb." It recorded their names and ages, and their physical and mental conditions, and it listed who had brought them there. "It made the children so real. They were individuals," Bauer says, "And they each had their own story."

The delegation also visited present-day children. They took a trip to the Buddhist center of the Rissho Kosei-kai, a long-time partner of the Unitarian Universalist Association. The Americans were welcomed and fed at their Dharma Center. And the Buddhist children performed for them. In return, Bauer presented the children with bamboo pendants with depictions of a chalice, the symbol of the Unitarian Universalist Association. Together, the bamboo and the chalice symbolized the meeting of East and West.

"The trip was meaningful on so many levels. It was so miraculous," says Bauer. She has done social justice work for decades and has seen how it has changed over time. "It's not just Lady Bountiful handing out Christmas turkeys anymore. It's more about understanding people and building relationships with them so you can make the world better."

The trip to Hiroshima with the children's art has inspired the delegation to ask what they should do next. "We know we need to be thinking more globally," says Bauer. "We know we want to be more involved in direct peace work."

That is certainly what A. Powell Davies would have wanted. Words from his 1946 sermon still resonate and have been revived for a new generation. And what he told his congregation after World War II is no less true today than it was then. He said, "The world is now too dangerous for anything but truth and too small for anything but brotherhood."

Pictures from a Hiroshima Schoolyard *(documentary film)*
www.hiroshimaschoolyard.com

"What are you going to do
that is important in your life?"

Resurrecting a Story of Holocaust Heroism

On a snowy night in Prague in 1939, Martha Sharp jumped from a taxi, darted around a corner, and flattened herself into a doorway. The heels of a pursuing Gestapo agent clicked past her. She ducked into an unlit apartment building, dashed up five flights of stairs, and rang the bell of a known anti-Nazi leader.

A woman opened the apartment door a crack, and Martha asked to speak to the man inside. The woman said she had never heard of him and began to close the door. Martha started to beg. She wasn't going back into the snow without the man she had set out to rescue. Martha told the woman that there was little time, and she produced her American passport. The Czech woman snatched the passport away and shut the door in Martha's face. For the next few minutes, Martha stared at the closed door, wondering if she would ever find the man or see her passport again.

But the door did open, and this time, a man stood before her. Martha asked if he was Mr. X, as she later referred to him when recounting the story. The man said he could give Mr. X a message.

Martha explained that she had been charged by a group of British and American refugee workers with transporting him to the British embassy so he could be smuggled out of the country. The man disappeared into the apartment, returning a moment later wearing an overcoat. He handed Martha her passport and said, "I am Mr. X."

Together, they walked through the wind and snow across the city. A Nazi soldier stopped them when they reached a bridge over the Vltava River. Martha produced her passport and confidently announced, "Americans!" The soldier waved them across the bridge. She produced her passport again at the other side, where a waiting Nazi soldier motioned them ahead.

A third officer stopped them just steps outside the British embassy. Martha began to loudly complain about the lack of taxis and her frustration with being late for a meeting with the embassy secretary. She flashed her passport yet again and demanded that the guard tell the secretary that Mr. and Mrs. Sharp were there. He waved them ahead to speak to a British guard, and Martha and Mr. X walked into the embassy to safety. Martha then returned to her apartment, where her husband Waitstill was returning from a similar mission. They watched out the window as Nazi soldiers looted Prague stores and warehouses.

Six weeks earlier, Martha, a social worker trained at Hull House in Chicago, and her husband, Rev. Waitstill Sharp, minister of the Unitarian Church of Wellesley Hills, Massachusetts, had been living outside Boston with their two young children. The couple had dropped everything, leaving their work and their children behind, to volunteer for a relief effort in Czechoslovakia, sponsored by the American Unitarian Association. But on March 15, 1939, the Nazi army marched into Prague and occupied the city. Instantly, the Sharps' humanitarian refugee operation changed into a treacherous cloak-and-dagger mission.

The rescue of Mr. X is one of hundreds the couple orchestrated, helping Jews and non-Jews, intellectuals, political leaders, writers, artists, and children flee to safety from the Nazis. Their actions led to the origin of the Unitarian Service Committee, which grew to become the human rights organization now known as the Unitarian Universalist Service Committee.

Yet the story of the Sharps remained little known outside their own Unitarian inner circle for more than half a century until their grandson, Artemis Joukowsky III, began piecing their saga back together. With help from his brother Michael, he sifted through thousands of documents across Europe and the United States, and tracked down refugees his grandparents had rescued.

Joukowsky presented the reassembled story of his grandparents to Yad Vashem, the Holocaust Martyrs' and Heroes' Remembrance Authority in Israel. And in June 2006, Martha and Waitstill Sharp were honored posthumously with Yad Vashem's Righteous Among the Nations award. The award has recognized more than twenty thousand non-Jews who risked their lives to save Jews during the Holocaust. Martha and Waitstill Sharp are the second and third Americans to receive that honor, joining only a handful of non-Europeans, and Martha is the only American woman.

For Artemis, the honor was about more than just gaining recognition for his grandparents' forgotten heroism. He hoped their story could spur others to act in the face of injustice. "I want to inspire a new generation of people to do this kind of work," Artemis says. "I'm interested in challenging the population to say, 'What are we going to do to stop the world from allowing a genocide like this to ever happen again?'"

What Rosemary Feigl remembers most clearly about the woman who rescued her from the Nazis is her hat. Martha Sharp wore a fancy one with a long pheasant feather. To Feigl, a thirteen-year-old girl with nothing but a suitcase to her name, Sharp was her elegant American savior.

Feigl had fled her home in Vienna with her parents in the aftermath of the devastating destruction of Kristallnacht. She wore a hat too, a beige beret. Twenty-six other children wore hats just like it as Martha Sharp led them across war-torn Europe to Portugal, where they boarded a ship sailing to the United States.

"Mrs. Sharp risked her safety and her life, when she didn't even know us," says Feigl, now an elderly decorative painter who lives in Manhattan. "She certainly wasn't Jewish. There was no reason for her to do it other than the strength of her character."

Feigl was not a political refugee. She was a Jewish child with her parents, who sought refuge in Italy, then in Vichy, France. She recalls that her father came across a network of Unitarians who were providing affidavits for asylum. And he heard about Martha Sharp, who was arranging to transport children to safety.

Feigl said goodbye to her parents in Marseilles. "I was so frightened of being alone. I had no money. I was going to a strange country and didn't speak a word of English," she recalls. Some of the other children were Americans being spirited back home. But most were Czech and Viennese. "They weren't all Jewish. They were just children whose parents felt the need to get them out of the terrible dilemma they were in."

Fifteen months after Feigl arrived in the United States, her parents followed. Feigl was among those who have paid tribute to the Sharps as the story of their activism has been made public once again.

The story of the Sharps' altruism and courage illuminates some of the dilemmas that face those who care about social justice. The world is so filled with pain—the Darfur genocide; the Iraq and Afghanistan conflicts; the global AIDS pandemic; natural disasters that have displaced millions in Haiti, Pakistan, and Japan; and human-rights abuses in countries around the world top a very long list. How many of us have yearned to go to the world's troubled spots and do our part, and yet have held back, uncertain how to balance doing good in the larger world with doing right by our families and local communities?

Taking a courageous stand does not require sacrifices and heroics on the scale of the Sharps. Rev. Dr. William F. Schulz—former executive director of Amnesty International USA, former Unitarian Universalist Association president, and current president and

CEO of the Unitarian Universalist Service Committee—recognizes the gap that many feel when comparing their own ability to act with the grand actions of people like the Sharps. Schulz says, "Not every one of us can visit the refugee camps of Darfur or the U.S. detention camps in Iraq or Afghanistan or God knows where else. But every one of us can be a part of the lives of those who do. Every one of us can be a part of institutions that make heroism possible and in that measure can claim a degree of kinship with the righteous among the nations."

Artemis has two hopes for what can be accomplished by telling his grandparents' story—one public and one personal. First, he wants their story to inspire others, not overwhelm them. "Life is made of righteous moments, not grandiose moments," he says, "making choices where you reflect on how you treat everyone in your life. The key part about my grandparents wasn't just one big moment. They made thousands of little choices that led up to the story that we now tell."

In particular, Artemis wants to call attention to the parallels between the Sharps' work in Nazi-occupied Europe and contemporary humanitarian work in the Darfur region of Sudan, where more than 300,000 Darfurians have been killed, and millions have been forced to flee their villages.

Former UUSC president Charlie Clements, who has gone on to serve as executive director of the Carr Center for Human Rights Policy at Harvard University's Kennedy School of Government, concurs that the Sharps' story is about much more than their past heroism. "It is our intention to celebrate their heroism and redirect people's attention on to the slow genocide in Darfur today. We want to inspire activism by asking, how will our grandchildren celebrate our righteousness in regard to the inhumanity that occurs on our watch?"

In his research, Artemis uncovered a large network of people who made his grandparents' work possible: church members and family friends who cared for their young children; legions of contacts of many faiths throughout Europe; fellow co-founders of

125

the Unitarian Service Committee, Robert and Elisabeth Dexter and Rev. Dr. Charles Joy; and Unitarians around the country who donated money to support their efforts. This kind of network is also needed today, Artemis says, to end the suffering in Darfur and in other chaotic places in the world.

Artemis also has a very personal reason for bringing the story to light. He hopes that the restored history will be healing for a family that came apart as his grandparents set out to save the world. His mother and her brother were three and eight years old respectively when their parents left for Czechoslovakia. Soon after returning to the United States, Martha and Waitstill divorced.

"There's no question that the work my grandparents did in Europe redirected their lives," Artemis says. "They were never the same people again. It's not a choice I would have made."

Some may view leaving home, church, and children as a necessary sacrifice, while others may see it as abandonment. The Sharps' daughter doesn't see it in such black-and-white terms. "My parents were extremely gifted, courageous people, and they really designed their lives around helping people," says Martha Sharp Joukowsky, a retired Brown University archeology professor. Her parents divorced when she was a teen, and when a judge asked her which parent she wanted to live with, she replied, "Neither one of them."

Martha Sharp Joukowsky recalls this matter-of-factly, without bitterness. "They hadn't really been my parents. We sort of raised ourselves. I came to grips with it years ago, when I was in my thirties with children of my own. Perhaps I am more like my mother than I think I am."

Artemis tries to imagine the way his grandmother would have framed the choice to leave her children behind. "She asked herself, 'What is a life worth? And what would I be willing to do to save it?' She decided that saving other people's lives and helping this terrible crisis was worth the trade-off. She knew her children were being loved and cared for and would ultimately understand that her being away from them would be understood in the larger context of what was going on in the world. But it was not easy. My grandparents made the decision they made, and they suffered about it all their lives. It's evident in their journals and their letters."

Artemis was in his early teens before he began to grasp the magnitude of his grandparents' accomplishments and sacrifices. As an eighth grader in New York City, he interviewed his grandmother for a school assignment. Their talks filled five audiocassettes, and his stunning report of rescue and self-sacrifice earned him an A.

"My grandmother and I became very close through this assignment," he says. "I felt that her story had some connection to what I was going to do."

From the time he was a child and into adulthood, Artemis remembers her asking him, "What are you going to do that is important in your life?" Even as a middle-aged, married father of three, a venture-capital investor in socially responsible businesses, a book author, and a philanthropist, he still hears her words.

As a child, Artemis always answered the same way: "I am going to overcome my disease," referring to his lifelong battle with spinal muscular atrophy, a progressive illness. He is an advocate for disability rights and is the author of *Raising the Bar: New Horizons in Disability Sports.*

"The influence of who his grandmother and grandfather were to him has taken shape in his life and grabbed hold of him and what he does," says Rev. Rosemarie Smurzynski, who was once his minister at the Unitarian Universalist Area Church at First Parish in Sherborn, Massachusetts. "I do feel that their spirit lives in him."

While growing up, Artemis had little contact with his grandfather. After the war, Waitstill worked for the United Nations Relief Agency in Cairo and at the Council Against Discrimination in Chicago. But his true calling was parish ministry, and he served several New England churches during the rest of his career.

Artemis got a chance to know him better while attending Hampshire College in Amherst, Massachusetts, a short drive from

Greenfield, where his grandfather had retired. One weekend a month, Artemis visited his grandfather and asked him about his World War II saga. During the war, Waitstill had concentrated on securing underground escape routes for refugees, about which little is still known. Waitstill had remarried, and he didn't speak much about his life with Martha around his new wife. "I would ask him about my grandmother when his wife went to bed," Artemis remembers. "He would light up, and I could tell he was still very much in love with her."

After both Sharps had died—Waitstill in 1984 and Martha in 1999—learning more about their story became a kind of calling for Artemis. He began to sort through thousands of pages of manuscripts and documents, including his grandmother's thick FBI file. In 1946, Martha Sharp ran for Congress against Joseph W. Martin Jr., a powerful Massachusetts Republican who became Speaker of the House the following year. Martin ran a smear campaign, insinuating that Martha Sharp's work to free opponents of Spanish dictator Ferdinand Franco in 1944 betrayed communist leanings. Martha Sharp was not a communist, says Artemis, but J. Edgar Hoover personally wrote a letter authorizing an FBI investigation.

She lost the election, but Martha later worked for the National Security Resource Board under the Truman Administration. And she continued her social justice work throughout her life. She helped found Children to Palestine, an interfaith effort to bring European Jewish refugee children to new homes in what is Israel today. She also served on the board of and raised funds for Hadassah, a women's Zionist organization.

Artemis also tracked down people Martha had rescued and aided. He traveled to the French village of Pau, where his grandparents had arranged for a supply of milk for undernourished children in 1940. In 2005, Pau honored the Sharps with the village's medal of honor.

Artemis uncovered dozens of new stories about the Sharps. He learned that his grandparents had rescued Lion Feuchtwanger, a prominent German novelist and dissident who was on the Nazi's most-wanted list, and smuggled him into the United States.

Artemis also illuminated details about Martha Sharp's 1940 rescue of twenty-nine children—including Rosemarie Feigl—out of Europe. Feigl related the rescue tale to the Yad Vashem award committee. In the process, she got to know her rescuer's children and grandchildren, and they have gotten to know her. "What happened to [my mother] as a child wasn't in vain," Artemis says. "When you meet someone like Rosemarie Feigl, who is such a grateful, loving soul, she is so clear that her life would have ended without my grandmother."

Never celebrated for their heroism in their lifetimes, the Sharps have garnered numerous accolades because of Artemis's work.

The church in Wellesley Hills, where Waitstill Sharp was minister and the parishioners cared for the Sharps' children, has honored the couple. So has Martha Sharp's alma mater, Pembroke College, now a part of Brown University, which celebrated her on Holocaust Remembrance Day.

And Yad Vashem immortalized the couple in Jerusalem's Garden of the Righteous Among the Nations. At a June 2006 ceremony, the names of Martha and Waitstill Sharp were carved into the garden's Wall of Remembrance.

Representatives from the UUA and the UUSC joined members of the Sharp family at the ceremony in Israel, as did Rosemarie Feigl. "My name is Rosemarie Eva Feigl," she told the gathered. "Martha Sharp saved my life."

Martha Sharp Joukowsky accepted a certificate and medal on her parents' behalf, and she spoke at the Yad Vashem ceremony. "It is good that this memorial we stand in today does not use the term heroes," she said. "My mother, trained as a social worker in Hull House in Chicago, and my father, a Sunday school teacher inspired to become a minister and lawyer, would be embarrassed by those labels. They were modest and ordinary people who responded to the suffering and needs around them. . . . They never viewed what they did as extraordinary."

Holding up the Yad Vashem medal, Martha Sharp Joukowsky said, "This medal not only reflects their determination and courage. It is about unseen efforts of a much wider circle of people who made their work possible."

Martha Sharp Joukowsky also acknowledged her sons, who spent years reconstructing the Sharps' efforts to present their case to Yad Vashem. "It was very emotionally gratifying to see my grandparents' names on the Wall of Remembrance," said Artemis after the ceremony. "It feels like the culmination of everything we worked for since we began this process over ten years ago. For my family it has been completely transforming to have experienced this."

The Joukowsky brothers were assisted in presenting the story of their grandparents to Yad Vashem by the Jewish Foundation for the Righteous (JFR), a New York nonprofit organization that recognizes, honors, and supports people who risked their lives to save Jews during the Holocaust. Stanlee J. Stahl, executive vice president of JFR, praised the Sharps and their denomination. "They went because their church asked them to," Stahl said. "Here you have a wonderful example of a denomination which said, we are not going to sit idly by and let the Jews and other political dissidents who are being oppressed by the Third Reich perish."

Mordecai Paldiel, director of the Department of the Righteous at Yad Vashem, reflected on the significance of the Sharps being just the second and third Americans to receive this distinction. "They left the peaceful environment and the serenity of the United States to go to a continent torn by war and strife to get people out," said Paldiel. "The Sharps didn't know what they would be up against. They had to use very unorthodox methods and place themselves at considerable risk."

Also at the ceremony was Rev. William G. Sinkford, then-president of the UUA. Reflecting on the ceremony, Sinkford said he had mixed feelings. "The first emotion—and it's a tricky emotional response for a religious person—was one of pride. I was so glad that our faith community responded to the impulse to help and so thankful that the Sharps were willing to put their lives at risk to do that."

"The other overwhelming response was that the tragedy that was the Holocaust could have been prevented," he added. "And that we, in our time, are called to cut short another holocaust, which is happening in Darfur, Sudan."

Artemis also sees the recognition of his grandparents' work in the last century as a call to action in the current one. "As we celebrate our grandparents' faith and courage today, we must all ask ourselves, how will our grandchildren celebrate ours tomorrow? Let the recognition of their heroism stand as a call to action. Let us ask ourselves, who are the righteous among the nations today? Who will take risks on behalf of unknown others now? We cannot all take physical risks, but who will take the risk of speaking out? Who will take the risk of bearing witness to the inhumanity of this era?"

For Artemis, telling his grandparents' story is a way to pass along the question that Martha Sharp posed to him throughout his life: What are you going to do that is important in your life?

Yad Vashem
www.yadvashem.org

Two Who Dared *(documentary film)*
www.twowhodared.com

Acknowledgments

I could not have written this book without the openness of the people who allowed me to tell their stories. I have been inspired by the vision and courage of all of you. And I'm grateful to each of you for allowing me into your work and your lives.

Thanks to the people who shared stories that inspired them and suggested people to profile, including Emily Graham and Rev. Elizabeth Stevens.

I'm indebted to many people around the country who housed me and fed me as I traveled, including Claudia Barker, David and Yooki Bates, Japhia Christos-Rogers, Tom and Sheri Lynch, Max Oeschger, and Jan Truslow.

Thank you to my editors at *UU World* magazine, especially Jane Greer, Tom Stites, and Chris Walton, who kept me supplied with a steady stream of fascinating stories to write. Some of those I have expanded into chapters in this book.

Thank you Mary Benard and Marshall Hawkins, my editors at Skinner House.

The support and confidence of my friends has been invaluable. Thank you Madeline Bartholomew. I know your sister Polly was with me in spirit, too. Thank you Dorothy Dunnigan, who has given so much to so many and Mary Scharzer Hampton, for your long-distance support. Many thanks to Suzanne Schwartz, who helped me spin out my thoughts, and Linda Croteau, Lynn Gallagher, and Jenn Tripp for your patience and encouragement. The support of my friends at First Parish Unitarian Universalist Church in Arlington was so welcome. Thanks especially to Angel Seibring, Stephanie Franzosa, and Mary Babic.

My dear friend Kathi Pelkey is a lifelong source of strength and humor. And thank you Elaine McArdle for your endless friendship and counsel in writing and in life.

I will never forget the enthusiastic encouragement of Jim and Doris Deakin. I miss you both, and count you among the writers I admire most.

Thank you to my parents, Ann and David Bates, for your love and for the power of your example.

I'm so grateful for the support and love of my sons, Adam and Charlie, and my husband, David. You are my joy and my spark, and you help me do what makes me come alive.

How to Get Involved

To find out how to get involved in faith-based social action work, see these and other organizations:

Standing on the Side of Love
www.standingonthesideoflove.org
> A campaign for people of faith that uses the power of love to challenge oppression, exclusion, and violence toward people based on their sexual orientation, race, religion, gender identity, or immigration status.

Direct Action and Research Training Center
www.thedartcenter.org
> Builds congregation-based democratic organizations that address issues from reading instruction and fair suspension policies in public school to accessible health care reform.

Gamaliel
www.gamaliel.org
> Grassroots network of faith-based organizations that are involved in political, environmental, social, and economic issues. Provides leadership training and leads local and national social justice campaigns.

Industrial Areas Foundation
www.industrialareasfoundation.org
> Helps create volunteer organizations from religious congregations, local labor unions, immigrant societies, schools, and other groups. Recruits and develops leaders to champion causes such as living wages and revitalization of cities.

The InterValley Project
www.intervalleyproject.org
> Organizes congregations, local labor unions, and communities to develop strategies to preserve and create jobs, affordable housing, and critical public services in some of the poorest industrial areas in the country.

PICO National Network
www.piconetwork.org
> Faith-based community organizing that tackles issues such as housing, health care access, school improvement, youth development, and immigration reform.

Unitarian Universalist Association Witness Ministries
www.uua.org/justice
> Provides resources and opportunities for congregations to develop their social justice programs and connect with other UU congregations and interfaith, community, and national partners in state and national campaigns on a variety of issues.

Unitarian Universalist Statewide Advocacy Networks
www.uustatenetworks.org
> Consists of eleven networks led by UUs that focuses on increasing the power of voice to facilitate change.

Unitarian Universalist Service Committee
www.uusc.org
> A nonsectarian organization that advances human rights and social justice in the United States and around the world.